REMNANT OF PARADISE

REMNANT OF PARADISE

ESSAYS BY ALICE VON HILDEBRAND

WITH REMEMBRANCES BY HER FRIENDS

EDITED BY JOHN HENRY CROSBY

HILDEBRAND
PROJECT

First Edition
Published 2023 by Hildebrand Press
1235 University Blvd., Steubenville, Ohio 43952

Publisher's Cataloging-in-Publication data

Names: von Hildebrand, Alice, author. | Crosby, John Henry, editor.
Title: Remnant of paradise : essays by Alice von Hildebrand with remembrances by her
friends / edited by John Henry Crosby.
Description: Steubenville, OH: Hildebrand Press, 2023.
Subjects: LCSH Christian life—Catholic authors. | Philosophy and religion. | Philosophy.
| Catholic Church and philosophy. | Essays. | BISAC PHILOSOPHY / Essays | RELIGION /
Christianity / Catholic
Classification: LCC BL51 .V66 2023 | DDC 200.1—dc23

ISBN: 978-1-939773-19-7

Set in Monotype Perpetua, a typeface designed by English sculptor Eric Gill
Typeset by Kachergis Book Design

Cover Design by Marylouise McGraw George

Cover Font: Monotype Centaur

Produced by Christopher T. Haley

www.hildebrandproject.org

Friendship is the remnant of paradise.
—Alice von Hildebrand

CONTENTS

PART II

REMEMBRANCES OF

ALICE VON HILDEBRAND

BY HER FRIENDS

FOREWORD

⁓

John Henry Crosby

The idea of a collection of essays by Alice von Hildebrand goes back a very long way, well before our close collaboration when she joined me in founding the Hildebrand Project in 2004. By then, "Lily," as she was known to her family and friends, had published numerous books, *The Privilege of Being a Woman*, *The Soul of a Lion*, *Letters to a Bride*, *By Grief Refined*, and, many years before, her *Introduction to a Philosophy of Religion*. But alongside these books, she produced a continual stream of shorter writings—essays, columns, letters to the editor, and innumerable personal letters. Often she would email me a short piece (and yes, she became an immensely prolific emailer in her late 80s!) that, as she would say, "I've just shaken out of my sleeve."

In many respects, Lily was at her finest in the presence of a live, in-person audience. I have one particularly vivid memory of when she spoke before a large audience in New York City, a little lady in elegant red who evoked breathless silence and tangible attention. She had this effect regardless of her audience. She could hold a room full of teenagers captive just as easily as she could command the attention of distinguished academics and clergy. Her brilliance as a speaker explains, I think, why she excelled in the essay, the written form that came closest to the naturalness and immediacy of speech. Her essays spilled out of her, much like the way ideas would flow out of her when she was enlivened by a conversation.

As her age increasingly prevented her from public speaking, she came to yearn for the contact with people that publishing essays online afforded her. While she often wrote for print journals like *The New Oxford Review*, *Crisis*, and *The Wanderer*, perhaps the majority of her output in the last decade of her life appeared at online publications, notably Catholic News Agency (CNA), which provided her with the joy of write, submit, and publish, often all within just a few days. Though she did not read the comments her pieces would generate, she would often ask me, "Dear one" (her preferred term of endearment), "how many comments has my article received?" Not a trace of vanity in the query, just a desire to reach as many people as possible.

Lily made no pretenses to originality; her love of truth was so deep that simply to discover and then share the truth was to her the greatest joy. She often spoke movingly about how each of us "deserves a patent for our errors," but how truth is never mine or yours but "ours." And drawing on Plato, she would often say that the goal of education is to "become unified in the truth." Lily gave the lie to any assertion that truth is boring. Her love for truth had a fecundating effect on her mind such that she developed original and characteristic insights into an array of issues, especially those related to the genius of woman and motherhood. In her magisterial three-volume work, *The Concept of Woman*, Sr. Prudence Allen credits Lily as a significant and original thinker: "Alice von Hildebrand exemplified the chronic vigor of a true development of the idea of the integral complementarity of woman and man in distinction from its corruptions, perversions, and decays."[1]

Lily was not just a gifted speaker and writer, she was also a rare personality. To meet her was to encounter nobility, reverence, love for the Church, and a passionate interest in *you*. Her famous memory did not just hold a vast quantity of philosophy, literature, and history (on sleepless nights, she and her husband would try to recite the kings of France from memory!), given a chance, she came to know and retain details about your family, the names and ages of your children, the significant moments of your life.

When we lost Lily on January 14, 2022, at the age of nearly 99, the outpouring of remembrances was a reminder of how vividly she lived in people's hearts, both those privileged to know her personally and those who knew her through the medium of print, radio, and television. This led us to include in this volume many of the remembrances written by friends, students, and relatives of hers. Similarly, we have included several essays on Lily that appeared at the time of her death. The essays we have selected, while

1. Prudence Allen, *The Concept of Woman*, Vol 3: *The Search for Communion of Persons, 1500–2015* (Grand Rapids, MI: William B. Eerdmans Publishing Company, 2016), 425-28.

in no way exhaustive, give a representative sample of the breadth of her output and highlight some of the topics most important to her.

Though it has been more than a year since Lily's passing, I still find it difficult to believe she is gone. Of course, she is not really "gone," just not here in the flesh. In our hearts, in the work of the Hildebrand Project, and now in the pages of this volume, she continues to be very much alive.

John Henry Crosby
February 10, 2023

NOTE ON THE TEXT

The essays by Alice von Hildebrand published here have been collected from many different sources. In all but one case, they were published previously, and the original publication information accompanies the essay. We are grateful to the following publications for granting permission to include them here: *America Magazine*, Catholic News Agency, *Crisis Magazine*, *Homiletic and Pastoral Review*, *National Catholic Register*, *The Wanderer*, and *Touchstone Magazine*. In addition, we are grateful to *America*, *First Things*, and Word on Fire for permission to republish essays about Alice von Hildebrand that appeared after her death in 2022.

The essays by Alice von Hildebrand have been lightly edited for clarity and consistency. Many of her quotations were from memory or from editions now lost to us. In this volume, we have used the Douay-Rheims translation for biblical references, and for the many quotations from St. Augustine we have used the translation available on the New Advent website.

PART I

ESSAYS BY ALICE VON HILDEBRAND

TWO SOULS, ONE FLESH

THE DIVINE INVENTION
OF MAN AND MARRIAGE IS A
PRODIGIOUS MYSTERY

Touchstone Magazine

January/February 2011

When at the age of eleven, I took a course on seventeenth-century French literature—French is my beautiful mother tongue—I made the discovery of Pascal and started reading his *Pensées*. Not only did he overwhelm me with the beauty of his style, but he also awakened in me a profound philosophical interest. I started memorizing many of his most beautiful thoughts, and I recall reciting them over and over again as I walked along the Belgian seashore where my parents had a summer home.

A portion of one *pensée* (72) deserves special attention:

Man is to himself the most surprising (*prodigieux*) object in nature; for he cannot conceive what the body (*corps*)

3

is, still less what the spirit (*esprit*) is, and least of all how a body should be united to a spirit. This is the consummation of his difficulties, and yet it is his very being.

It is simple, after all, to be just an animal, or even to be a purely spiritual being. It is so easy to be a chimpanzee: you are born, you eat, you drink, you reproduce, you jump from tree to tree, and that is all there is to it. Also, it must be marvelous to be an angel, pure spirit, without the limitations of a body. But we are neither angels nor chimpanzees. Man—whose complex nature deserves to be called a divine invention—is made up of body and soul so deeply linked that to be a human being does not mean to have just a spiritual soul or just a material body, but to possess both in a mysterious combination. The German language expresses this by saying that man has a *Leib* (body as subject), whereas animals have a *Körper* (body as object).

For man to have a body made up of matter that can be seen, heard, smelled, and measured, that occupies space, that is divisible and mortal, and also a soul, which shares none of these characteristics and continues to exist even after it is brutally separated from its material companion by death—this sheds light on Pascal's amazement.

Yet body and soul are meant to be so deeply united that even though the soul continues to exist after the body dies and decomposes, it "longs" to be reunited with the body. This is why I suggest that we say of one who has died, "The soul is now in a state of widowhood, waiting for the blessed moment when it will be reunited with the body." The "resurrection of the body" is an amazing dogma that sheds full light on the mystery called a human being. Indeed, God alone could have invented such an enigmatic creature.

Repeating and repeating Pascal's words, while the sun was setting over the North Sea, made me keenly aware of both man's complex nature and his fragility—like the sun sinking, we are heading toward death.

The Seal of Personhood

Genesis is explicit about this when it states that God chose to create man in His image and likeness. That is to say, from the very moment of his existence, man is a person, for God is Person. Man is a very imperfect person, but fully and truly one. One cannot be "more or less" a person. Either one is a person or is not. Those who claim that a baby at the very beginning of its existence is just a clump of tissue that only later turns into a human person are talking metaphysical nonsense. That implies that a being changes its nature, which amounts to magic rather than sound metaphysics.

Man's body is not an animal body; it is the body of a person. The implications are profound, for it means that every single bodily activity should bear the seal of personhood. "Whether eating or drinking, let us glorify the Lord," says St. Paul in his First Letter to the Corinthians (10:31). We are not animals linked to a soul; rather, we are personified bodies. Whereas both God and the angels are spiritual and have no bodies, man—this baffling being—is fully a person and nevertheless has a body.

This is what I call "a divine invention." I can imagine that Lucifer, the incarnation of pride, must have been outraged upon learning that God created beings that are as much persons as he is, but—horror of horrors for a proud pure spirit—persons incarnated in a body. Lucifer must have trembled with indignation at the thought of persons essentially linked to a metaphysical reality that is "low class"—a sort of metaphysical proletariat.

The closeness of body and soul finds an admirable expression in the Sacrament of Extreme Unction as formulated in the Tridentine Liturgy. It is now replaced by a very brief version called the Anointing of the Sick. What is strikingly beautiful in the Tridentine form is that the priest anoints the main parts of the human body: the ears, eyes, tongue, hands, and feet—all the bodily parts that might have been involved in the evil deeds of man. Because man is a person made of body and soul, his bodily activities are morally relevant. An animal cannot be either moral or immoral when it eats, drinks, or reproduces itself. Man, being a person, can.

Body and Soul, Man and Woman

Personhood unifies man in a very mysterious manner. Because our five senses give us information about the material universe (let us recall the terrible struggles of Helen Keller, blind and deaf from the time she was eighteen months old), St. Thomas writes that the union of the soul with a body benefits the soul. But let us not forget how much the soul benefits the body. Bears have a much keener sense of smell than we do, eagles have much sharper eyesight, and dogs an amazing sensitivity to sounds, yet neither bears nor eagles nor dogs can perceive beauty.

In a mysterious and amazing way, a human person is called, in every single bodily activity, to live up to his highly aristocratic title; in other words, man's body has a dignity that should be expressed in every single bodily activity. *Noblesse oblige*.

This "baffling" fact is still more complicated and mysterious, for in the Latin word *homo* we find a term that does not just refer to man alone without woman, or to woman alone without man. On the contrary, *homo* (which of course has associations with masculinity) also refers to the deep bond uniting two different sexes. No man without woman, no woman without man, is *homo*: they essentially belong together. This sheds some light on the pitiful confusion rampant in our society: the perverse belief that two men or two women can claim to be *homo*.

To be a human being, therefore, implies being both body and soul and also man and woman: persons of different sexes but equal dignity, and clearly called to complement each other. Now we see clearly why that baffling creature called man is so complicated: not only is he made of body and soul, but of man and woman. No wonder we have such difficulty understanding not only ourselves but others as well.

The Harmony Broken

Before original sin, the harmony between soul and body was perfect. They were like two musical instruments singing the same tune. There was also complete harmony between man and woman. Nothing can suitably express the terrible consequences of original sin. Not only did man freely choose to cut himself off from God—something he could not mend without divine help—but also, in well-deserved punishment, his body began to resent being personified. Man's animal instincts, which until that tragic moment had joyfully submitted to the seal of personhood, began to clamor for their own satisfaction, being no longer under the guidance of the soul.

This would have grave consequences. The resulting temptations were so demanding that, when not resisted, they made life very difficult for the soul. Temptations to gluttony, drunkenness, and sexual indulgence can rob the soul of its peace. Yet, if yielded to, these temptations inevitably make more and more demands, and, as a result, many a man soon finds himself in bondage to addictions, which can rob him of his moral freedom (cf. St. Augustine, *Confessions*, bk. 8). The conflict can be so fierce that man desperately needs divine help to extricate himself. He cannot do it on his own.

A further consequence of sin is that man discovered the fearful reality of physical suffering. The range is huge: from a splitting headache, to an agonizing toothache, to pain so severe that many are tempted to suicide. "Who will deliver me from this body of death?" exclaims St. Paul (Romans 7:24). In her autobiography, St. Teresa of Avila eloquently speaks of the crushing weight of a body afflicted by constant sickness. She declares her body to be her archenemy.

Many might assume that the body is the exclusive source of evil, but they would be wrong. No, the worst sin is the sin of pride. The soul can sin without the body, but as soon as bodily activities are sinful, the soul is involved as well. Of course, pride and concupiscence are often happy bedfellows.

When there is disharmony between body and soul, many assume that turning to the other sex will bring them peace. It is my firm conviction that if the body and soul are at war, it inevitably follows that any valid relationship with the other sex will be impossible. We witness this today: hoping to find peace, thousands of young (and not so young) people turn to sex, thinking that will provide it. So they "hook up" but are inevitably wounded, disappointed, and close to despair. This is why, according to Gabriel Marcel, we live in a broken world, "sick unto death." Two sick persons who "hook up" will end up wounding each other further.

The Remedy of Suffering

Holy Church, our loving mother, has remedies for these evils. Blessed are those who follow her wise counsel. Concerning bodily temptations, she has, from the very beginning, recommended penance, asceticism, hair shirts, discipline. Reading the lives of many of the saints, one is awed by their ascetic practices. In her autobiography, St. Teresa of Avila speaks eloquently about the severe ascetical life of St. Peter Alcantara: three small meals a week, a tiny cell in which he slept his few hours sitting, no protection against heat or cold, and even the striking of his own body—what is known as "taking the discipline."

Simone de Beauvoir accuses the Church of masochism: this is how a fallen-away Catholic—often the worst enemy of the Church—looks at these practices. Certainly we should never undertake them on our own. Our wise mother, the Church, makes it clear that such practices should be engaged in only under the blessed guidance of obedience. In monasteries, the superior or abbot is the one who should give his approval to penances that go beyond what the Rule prescribes.

Some religious orders still practice true penance today: the Carthusians, for example—the only order that was never reformed because it was never deformed—the Poor Clares, the Carmelites. But I wonder if, in some seminaries, asceticism, penance, and sacrifice are very often mentioned? Yet these practices work. St. Benedict used them, when tempted, by throwing himself into a bush of thorns. St. Francis of Assisi, the most popular of all saints, apologized at the end of his life to Brother Ass—as he referred to his body—for having treated him so badly. St. Therese of Lisieux took the discipline and writes that the pain brought tears to her eyes.

When it comes to suffering, the attitude of Holy Church is paradoxical. From the very beginning, she has advocated compassion and love for the sick, and she has established innumerable institutions to alleviate pain. At the same time, she teaches what many do not seem to know today: that suffering has a redeeming value. When we meditate on the death of our Savior, we should realize that, if properly understood, the Cross can bring us closer to Him who died for us.

Ruptured Bond of Love

Man's revolt against God was the first victory achieved by the Evil One, and it encouraged him to turn his attention to the love uniting Adam and Eve. Having himself chosen to exclude love forever, the envious Lucifer now aims at trying to rupture the bond uniting them, so profoundly expressed by Adam: "bone of my bones, and flesh of my flesh."

Lucifer's devilish wisdom taught him that sin would be the one factor that could separate lovers. To sin together destroys any bond of unity. Eve was to be Lucifer's special enemy, for her husband had called her "mother of the living," and Lucifer, being a murderer from the beginning, hated all life. This is why he launched his attack against the so-called weaker sex.

Alas, he succeeded. The guilty pair, after having first put the blame on the serpent and then on Eve, discovered they were naked. This nakedness symbolizes that they had discarded the beautiful white garment of innocence. They were rightly ashamed and tried, unsuccessfully, to find a remedy; they covered themselves with leaves.

Instead of begging for forgiveness, our first parents attempted to pass the blame, and they thereby created a chasm between each other. All the beautiful male virtues, such as strength, courage, chivalrousness, objectivity, and nobility, degenerated into their caricatures: brutality, heartlessness, selfishness. The same happened with Eve's beautiful female characteristics; sensitivity, receptivity, and other-centeredness degenerated into self-centeredness, vanity, and prejudice. I need not go into details. They are but too well known.

Greater Confusion

The greater punishment was given to the "weaker sex." She had been given the honor of bringing forth life, yet now this privilege was to be had at a high price: agonizing pains in delivering her child. It is noteworthy that when the Bible speaks of severe pain, it often refers to "a woman in labor."

In our broken world of today, this drama is clearly reaching a climax. Lucifer has achieved his greatest victory since original sin by convincing women that their privilege is in fact their greatest obstacle to achieving secular greatness. Crime of crimes, horror of horrors, millions of women freely choose to abort their babies, having been convinced that an unborn child is not a human being but a clump of tissue. How this clump of tissue magically becomes a human being—for to change one's nature is truly magical—remains unexplained.

Once this abomination became widely accepted, we

saw the inevitable consequence, namely, that the beautiful union of husband and wife began to degenerate into other confusions. Think only of the claim—rampant in our society today—that two men or two women can be married, and that this is their moral right. Sadly, the will to resist this aberration is getting weaker and weaker.

The Madness of Divine Love

Let us face it: The situation, humanly speaking, is desperate. The worst consequence of original sin was that man cut himself off from his Creator. The chasm thus created could not be bridged by man himself. God, who is Love itself, now chose to send His Son, the Second Person of the Holy Trinity, and have Him incarnated in the womb of the most perfect of all His creatures: "Behold, a virgin shall conceive and bear a son and shall call His name Immanuel" (Isaiah 7:14). We all crave greatness; we all try desperately to "ascend" from low to high. God—the infinite, perfect One—does the very opposite: "*Et Verbum caro factum est*" ("And the Word became flesh").

Kierkegaard, as always, found admirable words to express this unfathomable divine invention. He writes: "Christianity might be the invention of a crazy god ... so a man must judge who had kept his wits."[1] To go from glory to lowliness, to go from beatitude to suffering is the madness of divine love. Yet this is confirmed by Isaiah: "He had no form or comeliness ... he was despised and rejected by

---

1. Søren Kierkegaard, *Fear and Trembling* and *The Sickness Unto Death*, trans. Walter Lowrie (Princeton, NJ: Princeton University Press, 1974), 256.

men, a man of sorrows and acquainted with grief, as one from whom men hide their faces ... and with His stripes we are healed" (53:2f).

Mary, the blessed one among women, is by divine choice the cradle deemed worthy to shelter the God-Man in her womb. This mystery of mysteries opens the door to the reconciliation, not only between God and man but also between body and soul. For even when she slept, Mary's very breathing glorified God.

The Incarnation also opened the road to the possibility of a total reconciliation between man and woman. For Mary was not only fecundated by the Holy Spirit; she was also closely bound to the most silent and the most blessed of mere men: Joseph.

Let me end by daring to contemplate the holiness of the bond uniting them. Wisely, the New Testament says nothing about the tenderness, the ardor, the purity of their love. These are things that only in eternity shall we be worthy to contemplate. May the holiness of the holy bond uniting them kindle hope in us, for it gives us the promise that the bond established by God between man and woman can, once again, blossom through grace and lead to the glory of God.

THE DISCRIMINATION
COMPLEX

—◆—

Catholic News Agency
January 16, 2012

That the "weak sex" has been discriminated against has been the key theme of feminists. They claim that from the very beginning, women have been looked down upon as less intelligent and less talented (no female Dante, no female Shakespeare, no female Bach, Mozart, or Beethoven). History is the history of the great deeds of the male sex. Females are a sort of appendix, to satisfy men's needs, serve them, and produce children. There are a few exceptions, but the exception confirms the rule.

I have often addressed this topic and challenged some of its outrageous claims, but in all fairness, it is now tempting to look at the other side of the picture and examine whether the "strong sex" has legitimate reasons for adding its name to the long list of metaphysical plaintiffs. In other words, haven't men too been the innocent victims of "discrimination"?

Let us begin with Genesis. This sacred book tells us explicitly that Adam's body was made from the slime of the earth (2:7), then God breathed into his nostrils the breath of life. To have one's body made of dust does not denote a very aristocratic origin. Then God said: "It is not good for man to be alone," and He decided to give him a companion worthy of him. Any close bond between Adam and the animals would have been a metaphysical mésalliance, for none of them were made to God's image and likeness.

In contrast to Adam, the woman's body was taken from the body of a human *person* and made to God's image and likeness. Eve is therefore created "knighted." Why is this never mentioned by the feminists?

Simone de Beauvoir, the queen of French feminists, tells us that the woman was only a "second thought," condemned to be number two from the very beginning. She is there to satisfy the needs of the human male who needed a companion. She is denied whatever is great and noble, namely, to put her hand "at the wheel of human progress." Instead, she "only" produces children, something that a fertile hen does faster and better.

Be it remarked in passing that to be created last can just as well be interpreted as a sign of superiority. The rough draft comes before the final copy. But let us proceed with biblical teaching.

When Adam woke up from his sleep and saw Eve, his response was enchantment: "bone of my bone; flesh of my flesh." He truly saw her as a worthy companion, endowed with equal dignity and nobility. Moses does not tell us what Eve said when she first faced Adam. Being a woman,

I know that she too gave a response of joy for his "male-
ness." She immediately intuited that he was meant to be
her protector; she admired his nobility, his strength, and
his chivalrous character. She knew that they were complementary and made for each other. Metaphysically, they
are equal. Complementariness does not mean inequality, as
some feminists might interpret it.

Then Adam honors Eve with a glorious title. He declares her to be the "mother of the living." Can one imagine a more beautiful and more noble title, hinting at a bond
between God and the woman, for God is Life?

When Eve gave birth to Cain she exclaimed: "I have
gotten a man with the help of God." What is striking is
that Adam *is not even mentioned*. After all, he was the father
of this male child. But Eve gives all the credit to God. This
should give us food for thought. The father's role is crucial
but cannot be compared in importance to the mother's.

This has been strikingly formulated by Chesterton. He
writes: "Nothing can ever overcome that one enormous
sex superiority, that even the male child is born closer to
his mother than to his father. No one staring at that fright-
ful female privilege can quite believe in the equality of the
sexes."[1]

Why does Eve not mention Adam? A possible explana-
tion is that, unbeknown to herself, she was born a budding
theologian and is mysteriously alluding to the theological
truth unveiled in the New Testament, that God, and *God
alone*, creates the soul of the child, and that it is in Eve's

1. *What's Wrong with the World* (New York: Sheed and Ward, 1956), 198.

body that this "fecundation"—the crucial one—takes place and produces a human person made to God's image and likeness. Let us repeat: Adam is very much in the background.

Are human males not entitled to scream that they are being "discriminated against," and this in the Bible accused of favoring men from the beginning? Is it not high time for men to raise their voice in protest?

That the evil one addresses himself to Eve and not to her husband has a deep meaning. For once, I dare to challenge the views of my revered St. Augustine, who wrote that the serpent addressed himself to Eve because she was the weaker one and therefore easier to defeat. This is bad psychology. Being very astute, the devil knew that Eve had an enormous influence over her husband, and that the "strong sex" would follow suit in whatever decision she made. This is exactly what happened. He offers no objection; he does not remind her of God's prohibition; and he eats the fruit that she gave him.

Nietzsche made the deep remark that since the French Revolution, women have more power and *less influence*. The latter is more important than the former. Through power, one can "force" people to act in a certain way; influence is much more subtle and deeper: it affects not only a person's actions but the person himself. The "apostolate of being" (as coined by Dietrich von Hildebrand) is the best way of drawing sinners into God's holy net. One cannot "force" others to accept truth, but one can irradiate peace and joy and thereby "tempt" our neighbors to marvel about "our secret."

In contemporary life, now that many women take the limelight, they have much less influence on their husbands, children, and society at large than before. This is one of the very grave problems we are facing. Following in the footsteps of Esau, feminists have sold their birthright for a mess of pottage. Many female Esaus, who today play a key role in politics, neglect husbands and children, and contribute to the breakdown of the family—the very heart of any healthy society. Before the feminist poison had spread like wildfire, Charles Dickens in *Bleak House* sketched a perfect caricature of a grotesque female, Mrs. Jellyby, who neglected husband and children, being totally absorbed by her mission to improve the conditions of an unknown African tribe.

Simone de Beauvoir is right in stating that men have been the great creators in philosophy, science, technology, and fine arts. But she wisely conceals her scholarly dishonesty by refraining from mentioning the second Epistle of St. Peter in which the Prince of the Apostles states explicitly that the world will be destroyed by fire. No human creation will survive this universal disaster. The invention of the "bomb" makes this prediction terribly real. A powerful atomic bomb can, within seconds, reduce the world to ashes. Apparently cockroaches alone would survive.

What should be mentioned is that every single child to whom a woman has given life, having an immortal soul, will escape this universal cataclysm. A bomb can destroy matter, not the soul. Are not males, once again, being discriminated against? Their accomplishments are essentially time-bound. All their "works" will perish. There will then be a new heaven and a new earth, and a much better one.

It is typical of prejudice on principle, as exemplified in Simone de Beauvoir, that she is an expert at finding biblical quotations that are very critical of women. Let me mention just two: "I would rather dwell with a lion and a dragon than dwell with an evil wife" (Sirach 25–26); and also: "From a woman sin has its beginning and because of her we all die" (Sirach 24). But why omit the very beautiful quotations found in the Holy Book? "Do not deprive yourself of a good and wise wife for her charm is more than gold." (Sirach 7:19). There are many more. Selective scholarship is a subtle form of intellectual dishonesty.

Men who have caught the "discrimination complex" have more reasons for grievances. Being the "strong sex," why is it that the *great duel* is between Eve and the serpent? "I will put enmity between you and the woman" (Genesis 3:15). The same theme is echoed in the Apocalypse when the dragon and the woman are confronting each other. The male sex is supposed to be the strong sex, "the fighting sex," yet in the drama of redemption, the "weak sex" is in the foreground. That Satan's head will be crushed and that the woman crowned with twelve stars will play a crucial role in this final victory. Once again, the woman is assigned a key role. How are we to explain why men do not object to the fact that they are clearly denied the key role?

All these "grievances" are dwarfed when it comes to the New Testament. St. Luke tells us that an Angel of the Lord appeared to a young virgin, whose name was Mary, and in God's name offers her to become the mother of the Savior, the God-Man. She questions him, "How can this be? I know not man." Gabriel assures her that the human male will play no role whatever in the miracle that will take place in her as soon as she gives her consent. The Liturgy is explicit: "*Templum Dei factus est uterus nesciens virum*" (*vir* in Latin refers exclusively to the male sex). The male sex is excluded: "becoming Man without man's [male] aid."[2] Once again, the primary role assigned to the woman is strikingly formulated by the Liturgy: "O God who placed salvation in the hands of a Woman."

Where is the human male in this supreme moment? St. Joseph is not present, and is not even informed of the earth-shaking event that has just taken place in his betrothed's body.

This indeed is ground for feeling discriminated against. Moreover, this young virgin is the only creature since the Fall *born without the stain of original sin.* She is *tota pulchra* (all beautiful); she is the creature God loves most and will be declared the Queen of Angels, upsetting the hierarchy in which pure spirits rank above all human persons. She is the one in whose body God, through the Incarnation, is reconciled with man, for her blessed child is both God and man; she is the one in whom body and soul—at war since the Fall—sing the same song of gratitude; she is the one whose love for St. Joseph has reconciled man and woman, whose common sin had profoundly harmed the peaceful love that God had originally created between them.

The feminists who do not enjoy being defeated will

2. Dom Prosper Guéranger, O.S.B., *The Liturgical Year*, Vol. II, "Antiphon of the Circumcision," 376.

retort: What about the priesthood? This seems to be a formidable trump in the feminist camp. A few remarks are called for. *All women* without exception are meant to be "mothers" (whether married, widowed, not married, consecrated virgins). There is a metaphysical bond between *woman and life* established by God Himself, and this why any law allowing abortion (that is, a woman's right over her body) is the greatest Satanic victory that has taken place since original sin.

A very small percentage of men are called to the priesthood. God gives this honor to those whom He has handpicked for this unfathomable privilege. St. Paul writes: "But one does not take the honor upon himself, but he is called by God just as Aaron was" (Hebrews 5:4). When one reads these inspired words, one cannot help but marvel at some nuns who do not hesitate to declare that they feel worthy to be ordained. To say "I am not worthy" is a much safer road to God than to make the arrogant claim that, of course, one is worthy.

Being born without sin, Mary is the one creature whose very existence is not only a constant source of joy to God, but whose body and soul are sacred. Receiving the awesome sacrament of the priesthood does not make the priest holy, even though it challenges him to become holy. Nothing short of holiness is required.

Alas, how many today are conscious of this call? When the priest pronounces the words of Consecration, "This is my body; this is my blood," he is acting *in persona Christi*. It is no longer Fr. Brown; it is Christ himself who operates the miracle of transubstantiation. Man can forgive an offense done to him personally; but he cannot forgive sins. Hence the "scandal" of the Pharisees when Christ said, "Thy sins are forgiven thee." But priests who have received this ineffable dignity should pray daily that they might become holy, for the striving for holiness is required of priests in a very special way.

Mary does not have to strive for holiness. She is holy.

Moreover, every priest needs a mother; this is so true that Christ, the priest par excellence, has a mother, but no human father. Priesthood and maternity are so complementary that they cannot be united in one and the same person.

May these few thoughts open the eyes of the female Esaus, who feel that they have been discriminated against, and raise their fists against heaven, which has "only" given them the honor of giving life—life that, alas, some of them now feel entitled to extinguish. May God have mercy on a sex that so favored, despises the divine gift, and opts for a mess of pottage.

MARY, QUEEN OF WIDOWS

~~~~

The Wanderer

Mary is the gem of God's creation. For God made great
things in her ("*quia fecit in me magna qui potens est*"). She
has been honored as Virgin, Spouse, and Mother, but we
tend to forget that she also was a widow, and this is a topic
that we wish to address briefly.

She was married to the chaste Joseph, who was the
first to be informed of the miracle that had taken place
in her womb, the one to whom was granted the awesome
task of protecting and supporting her, the one who accompanied her to Bethlehem, who was present at the birth of
the Savior, the one who brought her to Egypt to escape
from the murderous plans of Herod. He was privileged to
accompany her and the Holy Child back to Nazareth; he
shared Mary's anxieties upon noticing that Jesus was not
with them on their way back from Jerusalem. He rejoiced
with her when the Christ Child was found in the Temple.

But that he was not present at Calvary—when the Holy
Virgin needed him most—tells us, without the possibility
of a doubt, that Mary was then a widow. His absence is not

even mentioned. Omissions can be very eloquent. Was it not fitting that he, who had shared her life in a unique way, should be with her at the foot of the Cross? He who, more than anyone, would have shared her agony?

God had other plans, and Joseph's absence is profoundly meaningful. God had decided that Mary—the one who suffered most after the Holy One—should also experience the pains of widowhood to give comfort to widows who, like her, carry the cross of loneliness. God had decided that she was to watch the agonizing suffering of her Son alone. St. John, of course, was there. But who could replace St. Joseph?

There are millions of women who share Mary's fate and have tasted the bitterness of losing the person with whom they had a tender bond for precious years of their lives, who had shared their sorrows and their joys. What a supernatural consolation it would be for them to meditate upon the fact that Mary had tasted the same bitter fruit of widowhood.

The Old Testament often mentions widows (never widowers) as deserving special care and attention. In the Acts of the Apostles, they are explicitly mentioned. It is a Judeo-Christian tradition that they deserve special care and love. And yet, surprisingly enough, the Holy Catholic Church has not honored the holiest of widows by dedicating a special feast in her honor. It would, I believe, be an immense consolation for millions and millions of Catholic women to have one day of the year dedicated to honor Mary as Patroness of Widows.

Women are often referred to by the Fathers of the

Church as the "weak sex"—those who need special protection, even though the Church knows that when they
love, women can exhibit a heroic courage that often fails
men. They came early on Easter Day to anoint the Sacred
Body of their Savior. Women are called, in the liturgy, the
"pious sex"—those who because of their frailty—being
more emotional than men and usually less in control of
their feelings—are blessed with a consciousness that they
need help.

To be pious means not only to give the proper response
to the holiness of God but also to turn to Him for help. It
is easy for a woman worthy of this name to say, "Without
thee, O Lord, I can do nothing." Moreover, the truly saintly woman would gladly add, "Without you, I do not want
to do anything." The Little Flower wrote in her autobiography: I have never been able to do anything alone.

The widow is humanly alone, but by humbly acknowledging her helplessness and grief she can, like Mary, beg
for divine help. To know one's weakness, to show one's
bleeding heart to the one who said, "Come to me, you that
are burdened, I will refresh you," are spiritual pearls essential to true prayer life.

"I am the Handmaid of the Lord; be it done to me according to thy word" is the motto of womanhood, whether married and widowed, or whether a consecrated virgin.
When Mary spoke these words, the immediate reward was
the Incarnation. Her virginal body became a sacred temple
that sheltered Jesus for nine months. In Mary, we find the
glorious beauty of virginity, the sacred bond of marriage,

the joys of motherhood (with matching sorrows), and the grief of widowhood.

May Holy Church add one more official jewel to her crown and dedicate one day of the year to Mary, Queen of Widows. It is certainly the wish of Catholic widows that the Church should honor this facet of Mary's life that, up to now, has not been highlighted.

THE CANONS OF
FRIENDSHIP

Crisis Magazine
May 2006

Friendship is the remnant of paradise. Aristotle sees it as
a virtue, and one's behavior toward one's friends tells us
a great deal about a person's character. That great friendships are rare is a sad fact that has been powerfully expressed in the words of Ovid: "*Donec eris felix, multos nu-
merabis amicos. Tempora si fuerint nubila, solus eris*" ("As long
as you were happy, you counted many friends. As soon
as the sky was covered, you found yourself alone"). The
beauty of true friendship—even if it is a rare jewel—shines
all the more brightly because it may be the exception. "A
friend loves at all times," Proverbs 17 tells us.

St. Augustine—whose heart was as warm as his mind
was bright—spoke beautifully about friendship. Friends
love one another; they share one another's joys and sorrows. "They enkindle themselves and they inflame one

another." They find joy in being together to share ideas and enrich one another by exchanging their experiences. As a teenager, Augustine developed a warm friendship with a boy of his age. The bond was sweet, and Augustine could not live without him. The young man became sick and, after falling unconscious, was baptized. Augustine was convinced that once his friend recovered, he would keep his distance from Christianity. But to his amazement, the very opposite happened; when Augustine started joking about his baptism, the young man warned severely that if Augustine wished to remain his friend, he should stop saying such things. Soon afterward, the sickness came back with a vengeance and the friend died.

Augustine tells us that his heart was "black with grief." He could not conceive how he could live without the one with whom he had developed such a profound bond. He wept, suffered, and shed abundant tears, but these were unbaptized tears. Years later, when Augustine wrote the *Confessions*, he remarked: "O madness which does not know how to love men as men should be loved." Deeply rooted in the Faith, Augustine perceived that any true friendship or human love should be rooted in God. It is only in Him that true love can blossom.

The wound healed slowly, but it did heal. Later Augustine was blessed with several true friendships; two names stand out, Alypius and Nebridius. When the latter died, Augustine wrote these gripping words, "Nor do I think that he is so inebriated by the fountain of wisdom as to become forgetful of me, for you, O Lord, of whom he drinks,

are mindful of me." Augustine finally knew true friendships because they were rooted in Him who is the source
of all love.

Friends share the same interests; but more than that,
each is so interested in the welfare of the friend that each
truly shares his joys and sorrows. A French author, Jean de
Rotrou, wrote, *"L'ami qui souffres eulf ait une injure á l'autre"*
("The friend who suffers alone insults the other"). He is
referring to the fact that friendship means more than enjoying one another's presence or exchanging ideas. There
are moments when a friend is in need: one's concern about
the other, one's willingness to help—if help can be giv-
en—will tell us how deep, how profound the friendship is.
Ovid's words point to the fact that many so-called friendships are in fact no friendships at all. To my mind, the
term "business friendship" is a misnomer. As long as two
persons have the same interest they will be much together,
enjoy each other's company, and fall into the illusion that
they truly care for one another. But in fact, it is only a
façade and will collapse as soon as their interests diverge.

The true friend is one who, when the skies are dark,
will be there to give his support, to share his friend's wor-
ries, and, if he can, to help him. To help a friend in need is
a source of joy for the true friend.

But how much should one be willing to sacrifice for his
friend? Money? Time? Suffering? "Greater love than this
no man hath, that a man lay down his life for his friends"
(John 15:13). When is this required? Is it *ever* required?
Here, some distinctions are called for. Since one can need

help in very different ways, each case calls for a different response.

There are people who, knowing the goodness and generosity of their friends, are tempted to abuse their friendship. They cry for help for insignificant reasons and do not hesitate to appeal to their friends' generosity for things that, in fact, they could easily manage on their own. The true friend should show his friendship by never troubling the other unnecessarily.

The situation of the one whose help is requested is different when, warmed by love, the heart of a friend always has a "superactual" readiness to help his friends. When he realizes that by acquiescing to a request he will actually "spoil" his friend, however, he should turn down the request. But—and this is crucial—this refusal should be done *lovingly*.

There are cases, however, in which a person will appeal to his friend's help because he is objectively in a difficult situation: sickness, old age, some emergency. In such cases, there is a discrepancy between the effort (or sacrifice) required and the greatness of the need (to take someone to the hospital in an emergency, to babysit for a mother who has several children when one of them must urgently be taken to the doctor). Not to ask for help in such cases, even though friends have repeatedly told them that they would be happy to help, is to "sin" against friendship.

A friend who refuses his help, even though the effort requested from him is small, and the need of the other is great, simply disqualifies himself as a true friend. The one whose request is rejected should sadly acknowledge that his "friend" has not yet learned the Christian art of true friendship.

There are, of course, exceptions, when the friend whose help is requested must turn down his friend's request—for example, when an equally grave situation has arisen in which he has already committed himself. There are cases in which bilocation is the only possible solution, but is so rarely available! Once again, the manner of refusing is all-important. It has been said of St. Francis de Sales that when it was not possible for him to accede to a request, he would decline so kindly, so graciously that the other person left him with love and gratitude. To lovingly turn down a legitimate request for legitimate reasons is even heartwarming: one feels that the other would have loved to help, that he is grieved that he cannot help, and that he will pray for the person in need. On the other hand, to yield to a "friend's" request, yet make him feel keenly that his request was a nuisance, not only can be wounding but also makes it difficult to be grateful.

The bonds of friendship involve no "legal" obligation. To the bureaucrat, this is the only type of obligation that he acknowledges. The beauty of friendship is that—even though no such legal bond exists—the friend knows deep in his heart that friendship involves a moral obligation that is no less valid.

The question is: How deep, how profound, how total is one's love for one's friend? How far does the "moral" obligation go? Tell me how much you are willing to sacrifice for your friend, and I will tell you how deep your love is.

Even though no one is obliged to sacrifice one's kidney to save another person's life, some generous people will do so because they love. A newspaper article recently reported that a man whose brother desperately needed a kidney transplant offered one of his own. Through some tragic medical quirk, the receiver survived, but the donor did not. Even though there was no way of knowing that he would die in the operation, the fact that he was willing to take this risk tells us how deeply he loved his brother. No mother worthy of this sublime name would hesitate to sacrifice herself for her child. Think of Gianna Molla, who brought her pregnancy to term to save the life of her child. She died shortly after the birth and is now beatified.

In ideal cases, the friend will offer his assistance before being asked to do so. As soon as he learns of the other's plight, he will joyfully run to his assistance. If his help is substantial, the other friend should hesitate before accepting it. Absolutely *never* should he view it as his "right" and be resentful when this dramatic help is not offered to him. Alas, our fallen nature tends to make us claim imaginary rights and be resentful when they are not "respected." There are sacrifices that can be offered, but they can never be required.

The way in which a person accepts help reveals a lot about him. Is he grateful? Or does he take favors and sacrifices for granted? I have heard the following remarks from people who have benefited greatly from other people's generosity: "There is nothing special about his helping me. I would, of course, have done the same for him." Or: "I do appreciate the time that he has devoted to me; but after all, he has nothing to do and is bored." Or: "It was kind of her to take care of my children for a couple of days. But she loves children, so it was not much of a sacrifice for her." Or: "He is just paying back what I have done for him."

One of the great dangers in friendship is to exchange roles, as it were. The giver should downplay his sacrifice: "I was happy to do so." And the receiver should carefully refrain from minimizing or demeaning the gift received. From this point of view, the desirable response of the giver should be the very opposite response of the beneficiary. Too often, however, people reverse these roles. Some givers like to magnify their efforts or their gifts, and the receiver can be tempted to play them down. This is unfortunate, because a generous friend will give with such kindness (and even joy) that it is tempting for the other to say, "But he was just happy to do it." With his usual mastery, Dickens has superbly etched such a character. Harold Skimpole in *Bleak House* exemplifies the type of person who refuses to provide for his own needs and always manages to find kind souls to pull him out of trouble. His gratitude is skin-deep, and he even manages, in a subtle way, to make his benefactors realize how fortunate they are to be in a position to help someone in need. Skimpole says:

> I envy you your power to do what you do. It is what I should revel in myself. I don't feel any vulgar gratitude to you. I almost feel as if you ought to be grateful to me for giving you the opportunity of enjoying the luxury of generosity. I know you like it. For anything I can tell, I

may have come into the world expressly for the purpose
of increasing your stock of happiness.

Of course, there are also persons who refuse to ask for
help even when desperately in need. They hate to feel indebted and much prefer to find themselves in severe hard-
ship than turn to their friends. However, once the problem
is solved, some of them adroitly (or not so adroitly) hint at
the fact that help would have been appreciated had it been
offered. This is a subtle and cruel way to make a friend
feel that he has failed to live up to the moral obligations of
friendships.

I have known persons who, even though in difficult
financial circumstances, prefer paid help to that coming
from a friend. After all, they need not thank someone
compensated for his services. I have also known some willing to help others but who refuse adamantly to be helped
themselves. Once again, they choke on the words "thank
you."

Another field in which friendship can derail is when
a friend spontaneously does something kind or gives his
friend a gift, anticipating that he will be rewarded by a
loving acknowledgment. There has been a time in all of
our lives when we gave something to a dear person, yet
his response was unenthusiastic. We had expected joyful
gratitude and were disappointed.

The fact is, there are right moments for giving, and
wrong ones. When a person comes home exhausted after
a long day at work, it is not the right moment to expect

a warm, affectionate response. We should patiently wait for a time when the other can be receptive. Moreover, we should not give a gift for the joy of receiving a warm thank you. We *should* give because the gift is beneficial to the receiver and refrain from being offended because we did not receive the gratitude we had anticipated. Even in giving one can be self-seeking.

Yet we should still wish that the other shows some gratitude, because gratitude makes the soul beautiful. This precious little word is one of the three golden keys of friendship and marriage. In our world today the sweet music of "thank you" is seldom heard. Years ago, it was so ingrained in the education of children that, as soon as they received a gift, they knew that they had to express thanks. Today the words are out of fashion. Consumerism has ruined this cord in the human soul: The more we get, the more we want, and the less we appreciate what we receive.

Gratitude is the blessed oil on which friendship and marriage thrive. there is, alas, a danger in taking for granted the numerous tokens of love we receive from those particularly close to us. We get so many of them that they often do not even register. But the words "thank you'" should be the golden thread that, day after day, weaves the precious tapestry of a loving relationship.

If a stranger goes out of his way to help us, we are likely to thank spontaneously; in our society, when this happens, we are pleasantly surprised. But if a loved one does the same act of kindness, it seems so normal that we fail to say "thank you."

Expressions of gratitude and affection cannot be said

or heard too often. Think of the sacred repetitions at Holy Mass. There are many of them (even though some have been eliminated since Vatican II), and they are so deeply meaningful. *"Domine non sum dignus,"* "Lord I am not worthy," used to be repeated three times. Can it be repeated too often?

When people live close together (this applies particularly in marriage) and see each other early in the morning and late at night—in moments of great fatigue and moments of tension—it becomes easy to say an impatient word, to be irritated, and to make reproaches to another. Only saints escape such dangers. There is, however, a timeless Christian medicine: to immediately ask for forgiveness.

It is said in Proverbs (24:16) that the good man falls seven times a day. Human life is a series of falls. But the crucial question is: When we have fallen, what do we do? To fall is not as bad as refusing to get up when fallen. And to get up is to ask for forgiveness and transform defeat into a victory. Noble friendships and happy marriages (they do exist, in spite of the defeatist attitude prevalent today) are characterized by the fact that one is always willing to acknowledge one's fault, one's weakness, and to ask for forgiveness. The holier a person is, the more contrite he will be about the slightest faults. This has been admirably sketched in Dante's *Divine Comedy* when he writes, *"Come t'è picciol fallo amaro morso"* ("How little fault to have such bitter force"). Which one of us is so hard-hearted as to refuse to forgive someone who is sincerely repentant? In some way, he becomes particularly dear to us.

This leads to a final canon of Christian friendship, the

unconditional readiness to forgive. To be unforgiving is to condemn oneself; for God cannot be merciful toward us if we are not merciful toward our neighbors. The words of the *Pater Noster* should be the object of the Catholic's daily meditation: "Forgive us our trespasses as we forgive those who trespass against us." Once I realize the immensity of my debt toward God, it should become easy to forgive others.

If someone very dear to me offends or wounds me, the pain felt should be mostly because the loved one has stained his beloved soul and offended God; the harm done to oneself should be immediately forgiven, and this very forgiveness will take away the sting of the pain. On the other hand, if a person dear to us wounds another, our grief should be doubled, first because he has hurt his soul and offended God, but also because we should feel the pain inflicted on the other, even if this person is in no way close to us. We should ardently pray that the one dear to us immediately asks for forgiveness, and use a loving fraternal correction to persuade him to do so. The fact is that the holier a friend or spouse is, the more he will be ready to say "thank you," to ask for forgiveness, and to forgive.

Friendship is a precious jewel, and Aristotle was right in viewing it as having the luminous glow of virtue. But how much more can we say of "holy friendship" rooted in Christ, sharing in His love for the loved one? Those blessed by grace, who live up to the Christian canons of friendship, will have a taste of paradise.

TRUTH: OUR DAILY BREAD

The Wanderer
October 26, 1967

If Socrates were alive today, it is likely that he would sit close to a newspaper stand and address the people rushing to grab a newspaper in order to "keep informed." Those who buy material wares, he would tell us, are highly selective and want to make sure they are getting the best for their money. As a matter of fact, they are likely to check with the consumers' bulletin in order to have a reasonable guarantee that they are getting safe and reliable products. But, there is no consumers' guide for newspapers, and we can hear Socrates saying: "What, you are about to confide your soul to a newspaper and yet you consult with neither father, nor mother, nor friend … ?"

Modern man buys newspapers as he buys bread, but he knows bread to be wholesome and nutritive. Can the same be said of newspapers in general? They sell information at a very small price, and given the modesty of the sum, people reckon that they cannot go wrong by buying them.

Newspapers owe their origin to the democratic belief

that truth should not be the exclusive possession of a small minority of well-informed people. All men should know the truth, and therefore, it is the newspaper's mission to spread it as much as possible, and at the smallest possible price. No doubt, this principle sounds noble enough, and is bound to carry the assent of all those who have resented the fact that knowledge had often been a privilege reserved to an aristocratic minority. Now, at long last, truth will receive the diffusion that it deserves.

He who keeps these considerations in mind will experience no small surprise upon reading the words of Kierkegaard, in which he states that if his daughter became a prostitute, he would never give up hope; but if his son became a journalist and remained one for three years, he would give him up as lost. How can the great Danish thinker give such a fearful warning to modern man, who considers his newspaper to be his daily bread?

The lines just mentioned are to be understood in the light of another saying of the same author in which he proclaims that, in every generation, there are hardly ten men whose greatest fear is to fall into error. But, he adds, in every generation there are thousands and millions whose greatest fear is to stand isolated, even if they alone have a true opinion.

Material things have an enormous advantage over ideas, for everyone will notice when a material work has been badly done. Alas, the fact that ideas are erroneous in no way guarantees that people will perceive them as such. Not all men are capable of detecting errors and fallacies. This is so not only because these mistakes are presented under the garb of truth or are introduced as "new" truths, but also because men's intellectual muscles are often atrophied, for, as we know, education mostly discourages authentic thinking. It was, I believe, Bernard Shaw who claimed he owed his fame to the fact that he had formed a habit of thinking once a week—thereby acknowledging that genuine thinking is a rare phenomenon.

Most men think so little that they believe they are thinking when, in fact, they are just repeating—undigested—what they have read in their newspapers, and insist upon their right of repeating it. Once again we are reminded of Kierkegaard's words: "They never use the freedoms they have but demand those they do not have; they have freedom of thought—they demand freedom of speech."[3]

A bad baker knows that he bakes badly. The man who has erroneous ideas not only does not know how erroneous his ideas are but will accuse anyone who antagonizes him of having himself fallen prey to error. We are indebted to Blaise Pascal for having seen and formulated this simple truth. In his *Pensées*, he notes that the sight of a limping man fills his heart with pity, whereas a limping mind irks and irritates him. It is so, he adds, because "the lame man recognizes that we are walking straight, while a lame mind says that it is we who are limping."

It is the moral duty of a newspaper to speak the truth. Péguy's words come to mind: "Speak the truth, the whole truth; nothing but the truth. Speak clumsily the clumsy

3. Søren Kierkegaard, *Either/Or*, Part I, ed. and trans. Edna H. Hong and Howard V. Hong (Princeton, NJ: Princeton University Press, 1987), 19.

truth, boringly the boring truth, sorrowfully the sorrow-
ful truth." Truth is the bread of the soul, but here the anal-
ogy with food ends. For whereas every man wants healthy
bread for himself and his children, not all men can say with
St. Augustine: "O truth, truth, how did the very marrow
of my bones yearn for thee when I heard them utter your
name" (*Confessions*, bk. 3, chap. 6). And Plato, while prais-
ing the greatness of truth, adds sadly: "But it is difficult to
convince men of this fact."

Now, we are in a position to understand Kierkegaard's
anxiety: Does the press give men what they need—namely
truth—or what they want—often error? If men preferred
poisonous bread to a wholesome loaf, the bakers insisting
upon making good bread would have a difficult time com-
peting with those desirous to please their public.

A newspaper is exposed to two grave dangers. One of
them is to tell people what they want to hear, instead of
what they should hear. This method has the obvious advantage of guaranteeing a wide circulation. But as Péguy
aptly remarked: "Flattering the vices of the people is more
cowardly and base than flattering the vices of the great."
The second danger is to cheat people into thinking that
they are doing independent thinking, while in fact their
newspaper has lulled their intellectual faculties through
the systematic and "scientific" use of slogans.

Slogans are to the mind what soporifics are to the body.
It should be clear, however, that the former is much more
dangerous than the latter could ever be. For they foster
the illusion of authentic knowledge and of having attained

a superior position toward the world at large. They flatter pride in making people believe that they can diagnose a situation by a single word. They claim to be concentrated wisdom, while, in fact, they blur a man's vision of the world and mislead him into believing himself to be a competent judge of every question. Slogans distort a person's sense for truth. It could be shown that there is a direct proportion between the increase in the use of slogans and the decrease in the interest in truth.

Slogans concocted by a small minority of intellectuals and disseminated through the press are subsequently accepted and swallowed by the overwhelming majority of men. They are presented in such a way that the public is shrewdly led to think that it has made up its own mind and is enjoying the benefits of independent thinking. In fact, the masses are being indoctrinated and rendered incapable of authentic thought through the scientific slavery exercised by the press. Against the background of these ominous abuses and dangers, the true mission of the newspaper shines up in all its beauty.

The remark of Kierkegaard's quoted above intimates that the prostitution of the truth is worse than the prostitution of one's body. But the evil that can arise through this intellectual prostitution is proportionate to the good that devotion to truth can accomplish. Indeed, few missions are as noble as the one of seeking truth and of spreading it when it is found. Few tasks are as important as the one of enlightening an ignorant and gullible public, and of helping it to gain objective information.

MOTHER ANGELICA'S
FEMININE GENIUS

⟶

National Catholic Register
April 16, 2016

Little Rita Rizzo was born in Canton, Ohio, on April 20, 1923, forty days after I was born. During the many times I had the pleasure of visiting Mother Angelica and appearing on EWTN, I always joked with her that "we were almost twins." Rita was also born thirty-four years to the day after the birth of Adolf Hitler. With that in mind, I always enjoyed reminding her that God always wins in the end. But she didn't need the reminder. She was living proof of that adage.

She was much appreciated for her sense of humor. She knew that if television had to be informative it should also be entertaining, and she was good at it. Witticisms flew out of her mouth without being planned. I recall that once, being on her show, we had a battle of wit: both having Latin temperament, we had no difficulty communicating. At one point, she said to me, "Do you realize that you are

very funny?" To which I retorted, "Mother, in Paris, one
would rather say 'entertaining.'" She had a good laugh. But
beyond all this mirth, I am convinced that once one came
very close to her heart, one would hear her weeping, like
St. Francis, because true love is so little loved today.

The word "defeat" seemed to have been written on
Mother Angelica's cradle. The child of an unhappy marriage, which broke down when she was a tiny girl, she was
deprived of the blessing of having a father. Her mother was
ill equipped to be a single mother and clearly had serious
personal problems. The child was raised in poverty and
total insecurity. The future was bleak. She was sent to a
Catholic school at a time when divorce between Catholic
parents was scandalous.

But one day, miraculously saved from a deadly auto-
mobile accident, she gained the certainty that Christ loved
her. This conviction—which she never lost—opened the
door to a new life. When she knocked at the door of the
Poor Clares in Cleveland, her credentials were "anemic," to
say the least. But Rita Rizzo, who soon would receive the
beautiful name of Sister Angelica, had taken the first steps
in ascending the mountain of holiness.

The superior who immediately accepted the young
Rita as a postulant must have been endowed with a supernatural sense, intuiting that this spiritual "beggar," so
poor in credentials and seemingly destined to fulfill me-
nial tasks, had a real vocation. Rita was committed to total
self-giving, lovingly embracing poverty (she was used to
it), with a profound understanding that a vow of virginity does not mean "renouncing" maternity but viewing

physical maternity as being too narrow for a heart fecundated by Christ's love. St. Catherine of Siena was one of twenty-five children. Mother Angelica, conscious of the wealth of her Spouse, thought that twenty-five children was too small a number. She wanted, like all saintly women, to have innumerable children—and God heard her prayers.

Convents are known to be impeccably clean, and Sister Angelica was assigned the duty of sweeping the place. Once her foot was accidentally caught in the cord; she fell and hurt her back so badly that, from that day on, she had to wear leg braces. Partially crippled as she was, she started to harbor plans that any "normal" person would characterize as "mad"—typical of "weak women," governed by their imaginations and erratic feelings. This was the response of the apostles to Mary Magdalene when she announced to them that Christ was risen.

The first of these mad plans was to found a Poor Clare monastery in the Deep South—well known for its total ignorance of the ABCs of Catholic doctrine. Money was needed for this crazy project, but Mother Angelica, having, like St. Francis, chosen poverty, never let money appear on the screen of her consciousness. She put her trust in God. She had given her life to Christ; what she planned was not her plan. It was God's plan—hence, it was his responsibility to provide.

Only a very foolish person could think that he could impress Mother. She was not impressed by any title, whether in front or back of a name, and could have intimidated Queen Victoria. She knew that those who declare themselves to be "handmaids of the Lord" were those we should look up to. And, belonging to the "weak sex," she also knew that it was the "pious" sex, the one that joyfully acknowledged its frailty and was never shy to ask for help. This gives us a key to Mother Angelica's life.

A deep awareness of weakness gives us a golden key to an amazing life where defeats, with God's holy chemistry, were changed into amazing victories. It should not surprise us that the holy women followed Christ to Golgotha: a woman who loves fears nothing.

Mother Angelica's supernatural qualities were the golden key to her "holy daring," separated by an abyss from self-assurance, which is often the downfall of many "machos," starting with the beloved St. Peter.

Mother's life can be summarized with the words "from defeat to victory." She refused to be defeated, putting all her trust in Christ, to whom she had given her heart.

When I dedicated my *Memoirs of a Happy Failure* to both Fr. Benedict Groeschel, C.F.R., and to Mother Angelica, I did not choose flamboyant words of praise. I just used two key quotations of our Christian life: "Without me, you can do nothing," and "I can do all things in Him who strengthens me." They could have been written on her tomb.

We should be grateful that someone, be it "only a woman," warns the world when it heads into what Dante calls *la via smarrita* (the way lost).

If someone had asked Mother whether she was conscious of the inferiority of her sex, I think she would have looked at the questioner with an expression indicating that she worried about his sanity. The weak sex married to the pious sex turns out to be the strong sex. Eve was created last, her body taken not from the slime of the earth but from the body of a human person; when Adam perceived her, his response was enchantment, and he proclaimed her to be "mother of the living"—a title denied him.

The most perfect of all creatures is a woman, the one who gave birth to the Savior, who declared that he was life itself. The Blessed Virgin Mother confirmed her place in God's plan with the words "I am the handmaid of the Lord. Be it done to me according to thy word." These were words Mother Angelica fully embraced throughout her ninety-two years.

Indeed, God has exalted the humble and humiliated the proud. History will tell us that this humble nun, who founded one of the most powerful Catholic media systems in the world, would have been the first to declare that it was God's work.

She was only his unworthy instrument—*Non nobis domine, non nobis sed nomini tuo da gloriam* (Not to us, O Lord, not unto us, but unto thy name give glory). Mother Angelica's amazing life clearly tells us that humility (*pauper et inops sum ego*) and a heart burning with love can conquer the world.

THE BLESSINGS OF
OLD AGE

~

The Wanderer

We know neither the day nor the hour. In our sick and violent society, in spite of the laws of statistics, no young person has any guarantee that he will see the sun rise to-morrow. In old age, however, this possibility becomes a certainty. One gets up in the morning saying to oneself: "I might not see the sun set today." The hourglass is emptying fast; one knows that one is on the threshold of eternity. Death, which is always a possibility, becomes a certainty.

In our society, whatever is young, healthy, strong, good-looking, efficient is glorified. The moment the merciless laws of aging find a victim, the latter will find it very difficult to find a job, or to get a promotion: he is "out" of the rat race.

The inevitable consequence is that, in our society, the fear of getting old makes many people panicky. The telling symptoms of "aging" must be hidden at all costs. This is why dyeing one's hair has, in the rich world, become a social necessity. A woman over thirty-five who does not dye her hair is actually looked down upon. It is very much as if she were not properly groomed. It is shameful to have a streak of gray hair. We must look young. We need only look at advertisements in newspapers and magazines. Most of them refer to "miracle" products that rejuvenate: wrinkles disappear miraculously, hair grows back. There is not one single part of the human body that is not the object of "scientific" research in search of "the fountain of eternal youth." Cosmetics sell by the billions.

Aesthetic surgeons are so much in demand that they can charge whatever they please, even though these "operations" are not covered by insurance. One's face must "lie" at all costs.

Years ago, white hair called for respect. Not only was it not considered "ugly," but it used to awaken in people a feeling of respect: the elderly possessed something that age alone can give. It is written in Proverbs: "the beauty of old men is their gray hair" (20–29).

There was a time when age was respected. Literature of the past (especially in the Bible) always refers reverently to "white hair." In the *Republic*, Plato does not allow young people to be heads of the state. In Rome, senators were *senex*, that is, men of a certain age. The fathers of the Church explicitly mention St. John's white hair. In Indian tribes, older men were those listened to: they had learned some wisdom. The rich white hair of Benedict XVI is definitely beautiful. Today, white hair is a symbol of death—something to be dreaded, something that we must escape at all costs. In fact, the wisdom of the ages teaches us that old age has something venerable: to come close to eternity should give to people a calm wisdom that enables them to judge events *sub specie aeternitatis* (under the aspect of eternity), with the proper distance, and yet with a profound feeling of involvement: *tua res agitur* (this concerns you). To take one's last steps in this earthly life is to realize how urgent it is to be ready when the Master calls, so that one can immediately respond: *adsum* (here I am), like the child Samuel in the Temple. I recall that when I was a child in Belgium, I never saw an elderly person standing in a crowded trolley car. As soon as she came in, someone got up to give her his seat. Today, if a young person would do the same in a New York subway, we would be taken by surprise. Why has this noble custom disappeared? The answer is simple: the predominant philosophy today is biological materialism. What is young, healthy, good-looking, fast-moving, and efficient is favored. Helplessness, weakness, physical flaws are looked down upon. The political forces trying to legalize euthanasia are just putting into practice ideas that have been taught in schools, colleges, and universities.

True, elderly persons cannot be baseball champions; they cannot win the marathon, but does this fact deprive them of the wisdom that is usually acquired through experience and suffering?

Moreover, if old age prevents us from physical feats, it certainly does not prevent people from making important and remarkable contributions in the arts, in literature, in philosophy, in works of high spirituality. Titian was still painting masterpieces when very old. St. Augustine wrote

The City of God not long before his death. His early works are the weakest.

The dignity of the person is not to be measured by his blood pressure or his blood count, but by the fact that he is a being made to God's image and likeness. It is high time that we realize that ruthlessness toward the weak, the old, the sick, and the unprotected (abortion, euthanasia) are the rotten fruits of Nazism. Hitler was defeated militarily, but alas, his poisonous philosophy has infected our society. Plato remarked centuries ago that to win the war does not guarantee that the winner is morally victorious. When the world—forced by evidence—had to acknowledge that millions and millions of innocent people had been murdered in both Germany and Soviet Russia, the response was one of universal horror.

Today, millions of innocent little children are slaughtered by those whose mission is to protect them (Wisdom 12:6) and we are no longer shocked and horrified. It is "legal" and therefore legitimate.

To be a person is to have wishes and desires. Let us assume that they are noble and legitimate. We pray for their accomplishment. When, for some unknown reason, they are not granted to us, old age makes it so much easier to accept God's will, trusting that He knows best what is good for us. How often in life do we experience that the denial of something we desired ardently—while at first causing pain—often turns out to be for our benefit. St. Paul wrote that everything turns to the good of those who love Him.

Youth tends to be intransigent. It resents the fact that

things are not as they should be. Promises are not kept; hopes are shattered; ingratitude is endemic; dishonesty is perfectly acceptable as long as one is not "caught"; beautiful friendships disintegrate; the wicked ones seem to succeed. The poor and helpless are oppressed, rejected, and even ridiculed. Legitimate and well-thought-out plans collapse. Disappointments can easily trigger bitterness and even revolt in a young soul. "It should not be, yet it is."

When one reaches a certain age and reflects upon the fact that we too have contributed to the imperfection of the world, we are given a chance, with God's grace, to become more patient and more forgiving toward the failures and sins of others. One accepts that we live in an imperfect world, a world of sin desperately in need of redemption. On the other hand, when we meet a true friend, when we witness noble and great deeds, when noble plans succeed, elderly people are much more likely to be appreciative and to say "thank you." Young people complain, rage, or even revolt when things derail; they often forget to say "thank you" when they are granted benefits or treated with generosity and kindness. Young as she was, St. Therese of Lisieux (she died at twenty-four) had already learned a great lesson. She writes in her autobiography that far from being irritated or surprised when nuns in her convent (whose lives were dedicated to God) said unkind words, broke the rule, or manifested their moral imperfection, she rather was joyfully surprised and thankful when she witnessed real acts of virtue. If this is true in a Carmelite monastery, what should be expected of the "world," let alone the political and the secular world?

History teaches us that riches are dangerous for us sinners. The most powerful nations have fallen into moral decadence, and this poison has always been the cause of their downfall. Our trampling upon the most fundamental moral laws will inevitably have dire consequences. Our rich Western society should realize that we are threatened by our very wealth and realize that money can be our downfall. We should listen to the call: *"Jerusalem, Jerusalem, convertere ad Dominum Deum tuum"* ("Jerusalem, Jerusalem, return to the Lord thy God").

THE JOY OF BEING
INDEBTED

⤙

Catholic News Agency
April 22, 2017

The word bankruptcy is a nightmare to finance people. Literature is eloquent on this topic. Consider Charles Dickens's *Little Dorrit*, among many other books: to be bankrupt is to be disgraced, to be an irredeemable failure, to be a good-for-nothing everyone has a right to look down upon. From time to time the headlines inform us that a titan of finance and known the world over for their command over billions has gone bankrupt, due to unwise and rash speculations, due to too great a self-assurance: "I cannot err in financial matters. I have a perfect mastery of this field." Quite often, crushed by their defeat, they take their own lives.

This brief essay is also devoted to bankruptcy, but a very different type of bankruptcy: the joyful discovery that we are totally bankrupt toward God. Indeed, is there anything that we have not received? But it is joined with the joyful awareness that our debtor is an infinitely loving Father, who opens His arms wide to his repentant children, whose eyes have finally been opened to their misery and who throw themselves into His arms. Indeed, there is more joy in heaven over a repentant sinner than over a just man who is not (or believes himself not) in need of repentance. The greatest victory is to be defeated by God's grace.

This has been wonderfully expressed by St. Augustine in his *Confessions*, one of the most admirable books ever written, and one that is addressed to God. Book 7 expresses poignantly the work of grace in the soul of a man richly endowed and who for many years had chosen what Dante describes as "*la via smarrita*" ("losing the straight path"). His rich gifts, not baptized by humility, were in fact one of the great obstacles to his conversion; brilliantly talented, he relied on himself and needed many years to realize that he was bankrupt. Thank God, he gratefully acknowledged defeat and burst into tears, tears of repentance and gratitude. Indeed, one of the great sources of joy is to realize that one is defeated by God's love and then to shed tears of gratitude.

How beautiful is it to be aware that "without me you can do nothing" (John 15:5), followed by the words of St. Paul, "I can do all things in him that strengthens me" (Philippians 4:13), which clearly imply that God expects our full collaboration. It is a theme that often comes up in this great saint: "I rejoice in my weakness so that the grace of God can triumph in me" (2 Corinthians 12). The lives of saints are eloquent on this theme. Let me just mention the Little Flower, who wrote that "I have never been able to do anything by myself" and rejoiced in her weakness. She always turned to God for help, and this sheds light on her admirable life in which every single step sings God's glory.

To be a self-made man—while not denying its merits—can be a source of temptation: "I owe my success all to myself. I am not indebted to anyone; hard work and perseverance are the keys to my success." Many millionaires owe their wealth to themselves. It should, however, be mentioned that to inherit a fortune also has its dangers. Man should always be on the alert because pride is not the only moral danger threatening us. Every situation has its own dangers, and the wise man is always on the alert, following the words of St. Peter: "*Fratres. Sobrii estote et vigilate*" ("Be sober and watch"; 1 Peter 5:8–9).

Sadly enough, life teaches one that many of us prefer to be "self-made" than to be indebted to others because they are allergic to gratitude and tempted to demean the gifts received in order to escape from the burden of this virtue rarely mentioned. If the gift is financial and has saved a person from bankruptcy, a beneficiary might tell us: "It was no great matter; my benefactor is so rich that it is truly not a generous act." Some will tell you that he had done the benefactor so many favors, that the gift is really only a repayment of long overdue debts. Others will tell you that the donor did it because it gave him a feeling of nobility, when in fact he was "flattering" his own ego, adding another feather to his hat. Or perhaps the benefactor highly advertised his generosity, whereas the truly generous person will keep this noble act to himself following the advice of the Gospel.

One of the most cynical proverbs I have read is a Hindu one: "Why do you persecute me? I have never done you any good." It is heartbreaking, and yet life confirms it. But the most cynical remark justifying ingratitude I know is the one of the talented Heinrich Heine, expressing his certitude that God will forgive him: "After all, it is his job" ("*Bien sûr, il me pardonnera; c'est son métier*").

Many are those who resent being indebted to others. It gives them a feeling of inferiority unbearable to their pride. They do not want to acknowledge defeat; they want to be in control and their own master. This reminds me of something my dear husband said, which made a deep impression upon me. Having escaped from Hitler's clutches at the very last minute, he and his wife left Vienna with a minimum of belongings hastily put into two suitcases and arrived free but as beggars in Switzerland. They were totally dependent upon the charity of Swiss Catholics. I recall asking my husband whether, having lived in a great villa for many years and now finding himself a beggar, he did not suffer. He looked at me with astonishment and said, "For nothing in the world would I have missed this opportunity of tasting the sweetness of Christian charity!"

I do not know which moral theologian first drew up the list of the seven capital sins. But late in my life, it surprises me that ingratitude is not mentioned, a sin that goes back to our first parents, and, alas, plays a great role in our poor human lives. Ingratitude. It is certainly one of the very ugly sins, but how many of us are aware of it and mention it when we confess our sins?

May these few remarks be a clarion call to all of us to pray: "Give me a grateful heart, O Lord," that I may join the angels whose song is gratitude to God's gift of being.

TRUTH OR CHARITY?

Homiletic and Pastoral Review
April 2007

One of the most burning topics today is the relationship between "truth" and "charity." I shall defend the thesis that they are so closely linked that they cannot be severed. It is, however, fashionable today to establish a dichotomy between them. "Tolerance" and "compassion" are politically correct. The word "truth" jars modern ears: it is redolent of authoritarianism. Many of my students were clearly allergic to the very word. How right Pope Benedict XVI was when he spoke of "dictatorial relativism." Unfortunately, a democratic majority can also be "dictatorial." In the nineteenth century, the megalomaniac Auguste Comte had already proclaimed, "Everything is relative, except the statement itself."

Before coming to the core of this article—the bond between truth and charity—a few remarks are called for. It would be a mistake to believe that up to recent times men were always receptive toward truth, and in this context I am referring to moral and religious truth. In his last work—*The Laws*—Plato wrote that men "prefer themselves to the truth" (5.732). Obviously, they are not tempted to prefer themselves to "neutral" truths, and I mean by "neutral" those that have no bearing on the way we should live. In my long career, I have never met anyone opposed to geometrical conclusions. My students usually would defend the thesis that these command universal agreement because they are "factual" and therefore "certain," whereas philosophical views are only "opinions"—and why should one opinion be better than another? It sounds convincing enough, but the real reason is quite different, namely, that geometrical truths do not affect us personally; they do not dictate how we should live. It would be odd, indeed, if someone had a nervous breakdown upon finding out that the sum of the angles of a triangle are equal to two right angles. But I had a student who declared—very emotionally and with tragic honesty—that the worst thing that could happen to him would be to discover that he had an immortal soul—because then "I would be accountable for my way of living." Needless to say, my chances of convincing him that he was mistaken were nonexistent: one never sees what one does not want to see. The question is not "Is it a convincing argument?" but, rather, "Is one willing to be convinced by its validity?"

On the other hand, deep down men have a longing for truth. Let us recall St. Augustine at age nineteen reading Cicero's *Hortensius* and exclaiming: "O truth, truth, how did the very marrow of my bones yearn for thee when I heard them utter your name" (*Confessions*, bk. 3, chap. 6). Man is full of contradictions, and oftentimes there is a battle in his soul between this thirst for truth, and simultaneously the fear of having to follow its dictates: "Not yet today; tomorrow," exclaimed Augustine shortly before his conversion. How many of us can be certain that we will have a tomorrow?

The "unsavory" word "truth" is replaced today by "interesting," "new," "challenging," "modern," "up to date." In C. S. Lewis's *Screwtape Letters*, the master devil recommends his pupil to eliminate the word "truth" altogether and replace it by the words just mentioned. The psychological recipe works.

In a book written shortly before his death, Jacques Maritain deplored the contemporary "indifference to truth" (*De l'Eglise du Christ*, 1970). This is grave indeed for man's personal life, for his moral life, and most of all for his religious life. Among all the religious founders, Christ is the only one who said "I am the Truth." Neither Buddha, nor Moses, nor Muhammad has dared utter such words. This assertion can be validly pronounced only by God himself. This is why Roman Catholics gratefully accept the official teachings of Holy Church, because Christ gave the keys of the Church to St. Peter, and she alone has the fullness of revelation. St. Paul warned us that truth will become unpalatable to many: "For there shall be a time, when they will not endure sound doctrine" (2 Timothy 4:3). Kierkegaard wrote in his *Journals*: "Every man is more or less afraid of the truth." [1] This is why self-knowledge is so difficult to attain. It is fearful to see oneself in the light

1. *The Journals of Kierkegaard*, ed. and trans. Alexander Dru (New York: Harper, 1959), 202.

of God. *Who, O Lord, is innocent? Who can sustain the divine sight?*

The unpopularity of the Roman Catholic Church is partially due to the fact that she claims, from her very birth, that she is the one true Church—a claim that is viewed as scandalously arrogant. What about other "points of view"? Why this pretentious claim that she alone has the fullness of divine revelation?

Up to Vatican II, this holy claim was loudly proclaimed. Today, it is seldom, if ever, asserted from the pulpit. This assertion is definitely against the Zeitgeist that advocates "broadness of views," "open-mindedness," and what my husband dubbed "ecumenitis." Truth is considered "divisive," whereas the word "opinion" brings men together. A very orthodox Jewish colleague of mine defined ecumenism (as understood by most) as the meeting of an atheistic Jew with a fallen-away Roman Catholic, and their pleasant discovery "that they have much in common."

According to some interpretations of Vatican II, the Roman Catholic Church has finally caught up with the time, which is opposed to any claim to the full possession of revealed truth. The reasoning behind this view is: How are we to attain peace in a world torn by religious conflicts? Is it not more reasonable to say that all religions are ways to God, and that truth being relative, each one of them has a message valid for certain cultures at certain times? Man "having come of age" realizes that to accept the validity of all positions is the way to universal harmony and peace: no more religious wars, no more bickering over hairsplitting distinctions that no one cares about anyway.

A new, broad road is opened to us: the new age of universal peace. One thing is obvious: the word "truth" has to be eliminated altogether; for this short word is a mine of potential conflicts.

Is that "true" ecumenism? Does it require the elimination of the key word of human existence—Truth—in the name of tolerance and charity?

The prayer of Christ "that all may be one" is a wish that all of us should take to heart: "It is beautiful indeed when brothers live in unity" (Psalm 133). It should be our ardent prayer. But it is sheer illusion to believe that true unity can be achieved if truth is eliminated.

The amazing and glorious Christian message—realized in the Incarnation—is that God is both Truth *and* Love. Christ claimed that He was the Truth; St. John tells us that God is Love. No other religion has united Truth and Love as two essential perfections of God Himself. They are two facets of the glorious supernatural reality that flows out of the miracle of God's love: the Incarnation. To sever one of these divine attributes from the other is to create a split in the Divine Person. How can our ardent love for our brothers be better expressed than in our burning desire to share with them the plenitude of Truth found in Him who is Love and has the Church as His Bride? To "love" others without this ardent wish to have them find the plenitude of Truth is to misunderstand the nature of love. To create a dichotomy between Truth and Love, which are one in Christ, is to lose sight of the supernatural and fall back into a humanitarianism—a poor human substitute for divine love—a "love" stripped of its supernatural perfume.

Those who through God's grace would gladly give their lives for the One True Church ardently desire that all men—without exception—would accept Christ as God and the Holy Catholic Church as His Holy Bride. But how should they communicate this message? No doubt, because men are imperfect, they can, in spite of their good intentions, create obstacles to the reception of their true message. What are the virtues that a true apostle should possess? What are the dangers lurking in the apostolate?

Let me mention some of the most obvious ones. The greatest caricature of a true missionary spirit is the shocking and grotesque attitude of those who try to force truth upon others. To proclaim with a club in hand that "God is love" is pathetically comical. This is an abomination that has, alas, taken place in history, rich in every possible type of abuse. He who wishes to help another to see a truth should approach him with loving reverence, and carefully avoid an "arrogant triumphalism," an attitude that betrays the pride of the one who has the truth. Truth makes one humble, not proud. *Such a person behaves very much as if truth were his own possession that he generously offers to others.* The very essence of fanaticism is to view truth as one's own possession and resent the fact that others do not accept it. It is taken as a personal offense. Cardinal Newman wrote that "others are so intemperate and intractable that there is no greater calamity for a good cause than that they should get hold of it" (*Idea of a University*). We must dread a poisoned zeal—the evil zeal referred to by St. Benedict in his Rule (72). This zeal is animated by the eagerness to conquer through one's own strength, so that one can receive full credit for the victory. This danger has been admirably diagnosed by Kierkegaard in his book *Purity of Heart*. How many so-called apostles reformulate the words of St. John the Baptist according to their own vanity: instead of saying, "May He increase and I diminish," they choose to say, "May He increase and I with Him." How crucial it is for the true apostle to meditate on St. Luke's Gospel reminding us that when we have fulfilled our duty, we should remember that we are useless servants. "*Non nobis Domine, non nobis, sed nomini tuo da gloriam*," "Not to us Lord, not to us, but to Your Name be the Glory" (Psalm 113), should be words in the heart and on the lips of every true apostle. God does not need us, and when He calls us to collaborate with Him, we should beg Him that He would—for a brief moment—put our faults in bracket so that they would not create an obstacle to the beloved soul in search of truth.

Another widespread danger is what Dietrich von Hildebrand calls "a lack of discretion"—a virtue of key importance in the apostolate and often forgotten or very little respected. Solomon proclaimed that there is time for speaking and a time for silence. There should always be a time for prayer. There is a right moment, and there is a wrong moment; to decide how soon grace should blossom in another soul is to put roadblocks to conversion. To pick up a fruit before it is ripe is to ruin it.

There must be a reverent listening into another person's soul to know the moment when truth should be communicated. But how does this square with St. Paul's command that we should preach the truth "in season and out of season"? These words coming from the mouth of

an apostle must be taken seriously. Never should our loving concern about our neighbor be relegated to the background of our preoccupations, but one can communicate
the divine message in various ways: one of them is by ardent but silent prayer. Another one is by the "apostolate of
being"—the gentle radiation of peace and joy that is the
secret of the saint. Another one is by the spoken or written word when this word is the fruit of grace. It was Plato
who wrote, "We must dare speak the truth when truth is
our theme." The words that first stand out are "we must
dare," implying clearly that to utter certain unpalatable
truths is dangerous. The second is that Plato tells us that
there is a time when truth is the theme and must be addressed openly, and there are moments in which it must
be kept in one's heart because the right moment has not
come. We must patiently wait for the right signal that can
be perceived when we are recollected, and the hearer is
willing to listen.

Christianity is unique in its claim that truth and charity are one: to communicate truth without charity is to
inject some poison in it. To believe that one is "charitable" by eliminating truth for fear of displeasing others is a
betrayal of both truth and authentic charity. It is a cheap
way of being popular and accepted by everybody. There is
a luminous passage in the Gospel that states clearly that
truth cannot be severed from love. When Christ chases a
devil from a man possessed, and the man exclaims, "Thou
art the Christ, the Son of the living God," Christ, to our
amazement, forbids him to say so. In the light of what we
have just discussed it becomes luminously clear that the

Evil One, when proclaiming the key Truth of Christianity, does it without charity, of which he is forever deprived: the Evil One knows the Truth, but this knowledge is totally severed from love and is therefore poisoned. To proclaim truth without love is to insert a subtle poison in the nectar of truth. Conversely, to believe that there can be true charity without a passionate love for Truth and an ardent desire to share it with those who do not have it is a false charity, stripped of its innermost core. To refrain from communicating truth out of "love" is a plain betrayal. The inseparable union of truth and charity is the very foundation of Christianity. To claim that by eliminating truth—a potential source of disagreement—we can truly love is to lie to oneself and to cheat others. The dichotomy that some well-meaning Christians have established between these two pillars of our faith is a tragic human deviation that must be diagnosed as a grave betrayal of Christ's message.

Missionary zeal animated by love is essential to Roman Catholicism. But man's talent for listening "halfway" is so remarkable that today many assume that true charity eliminates a concern for truth because some truths are unpalatable. Dialogue has its value, but it should not replace a fulfillment of Christ's command: "Go and teach all nations." Teaching is not dialoguing: It is proclaiming truth in His name. But this "teaching" should be rooted in an ardent, burning love for the sheep that are living in error, or in partial error. If we benefit from the totality of revelation—found alone in its fullness in the Holy Catholic Church—it is our duty to share it: we have no right to keep to ourselves a treasure that belongs to all men. Granted

that a positive relationship can be established between
people of different faiths, for all of them are children of
the same God, this is only a first step, aiming at destroying
their deeply rooted prejudices, aiming at making them realize that we love them in Christ, and that we are anxious
to share with them the gifts we have received. To quote
Dietrich von Hildebrand: "There are only two types of
men: Catholics *in re* (in reality), Catholics *in spe* (in hope),"
(those who are already Catholics and those who are pro-
spective Catholics). This will be realized in heaven.

Let me repeat: those called to the apostolate should
always pray, "I am an unworthy instrument; give me the
grace—when I approach strayed sheep—to put my faults
in brackets for a short while, so that what comes 'from
You through me' is not poisoned by my imperfections."
How different this is from the attitude of those who betray
their faith in the erroneous belief that the elimination of
truth is required by compassionate love. It is tempting and
fashionable to nourish the illusion that differences between
various religions are "insignificant" by comparison with
what unites them and should in fact be overlooked. But is
it insignificant to believe that Christ is God or to reject it?
That God is a Trinity of persons or that it is not the case?
Is it unimportant to believe or not to believe that Christ is
present in the Holy Eucharist? Is it unimportant to accept
the authority of St. Peter or to reject it? Is it unimportant
to be either monotheistic or polytheistic? Is it indifferent
to believe in personal immortality, or to believe that either there is no immortality or that we shall all melt into
a huge unknown?

Plato wrote that the gravity of an error depends upon the object we are erring about. To confuse a mule with a horse is regrettable but insignificant. But, he tells us, we should give our greatest and fullest attention to avoiding mistakes in the domain which matters most: God (or the gods) and His relationship to man (*The Laws*, 7.803). This is precisely the domain in which the words of Kierkegaard tragically apply: "No, to be in error or delusion is (quite un-Socratically) the thing they fear the least,"[2] and obviously he is referring to the ethical and religious sphere. I have heard *ad nauseam*, "What does it matter what a person believes if he feels good about it and it makes him happy?" Tolerance can be an "unsacred" veil covering indifference toward the beliefs of others. Basically, it repeats the words of Cain: "Am I my brother's keeper?" Yes, I am.

Another misconception that has gained currency is the exclusive concern with salvation. More than once, Protestants have asked me whether I was saved. Upon my telling them that trusting in God's grace, I hope to go to heaven, they would look at me with pity, for they have the guarantee that they are saved.

The Church has always taught that those that are victims of "invincible" ignorance, those who have had no chance of hearing the blessed song of revelation, those who are totally ignorant of the divine message and live according to their conscience and follow the natural law, can be saved. To many Catholics today, this clearly frees them

2. Søren Kierkegaard, *Fear and Trembling* and *The Sickness Unto Death*, ed. and trans. Walter Lowrie (Princeton, NJ: Princeton University Press, 1974), 176.

from their obligation to share Truth with their brothers. "They can be saved; why should I bother?" What they forget is that according to Catholic teaching, the glorification of God is the primary end of man; beatitude is the second. Christ said to the Samaritan woman that we should adore God "in spirit and in truth." To render to God the honor He deserves we must know who He is, and how are we to know it if it is not revealed to us?

Our model should be the missionary apostle *par excellence*: St. Paul, the Apostle of the Gentiles, thanks to whose heroic work the pagan world heard the divine message. From the moment of his miraculous conversion on his way to Damascus, to the moment of his holy death, while facing the greatest obstacles, whether hunger, cold, persecutions, beatings, shipwreck, or threats of death, he dedicated every moment of his life to preaching the word of God. But this did not allow him to forget for a moment his brothers in the flesh—those who had refused to hear his message. His love for them finds its expression in his Epistle to the Romans, in which we read the amazing words, the most ardent expression of love: "I have great sorrow and unceasing anguish in my heart" (9:2–3). And he adds the amazing words, the ultimate expression of the holy madness of love, that he would wish himself to be accursed for the sake of his brothers.

Let us pray ardently to St. Paul that he may grant us his ardor in understanding that to share the Truth is the greatest gift of true Love.

ST. AUGUSTINE AND TEARS

~

The Wanderer

To analyze tears is a fascinating topic. Many are those who identify tears with softness, sentimentality, weakness, and self-centeredness, and look down upon women who, more than men, often cry. Surprisingly enough, they forget that the Gospels tell us that the Savior of the world, the Man of Sorrow, wept twice. First when facing Jerusalem: "Thou hast not known the time of thy visitation" (Luke 19:44). When He stood in front of Lazarus' tomb, knowing that He had the power to raise him from the dead, He also shed tears. This is proof enough that to weep does not necessarily indicate weakness and sentimentality. There are tears of rage, there are tears caused by pain; there are tears of love and gratitude. Some of them reveal an evil heart; some of them have the ring of nobility and tenderness of heart.

In this context I shall limit myself to meditating briefly on St. Augustine's *Confessions*. He cried before his conversion; he wept at the very moment of his conversion. He shed tears after his conversion. What do these tears tell us?

At the very beginning of *Confessions*, Augustine tells us that he wept when reading Virgil's *Aeneid* relating Dido's suicide. Aeneas had departed from her, never to come back. Augustine condemns these tears, which—while enjoyable—were responding to an imaginary grief that pleasantly tickled the cords of the human heart. These were wasted tears. Augustine writes that there was a tragic contrast between his artificial tenderness, for a nonexistent woman. "For what can be more wretched than the wretch who pities not himself shedding tears over the death of Dido for love of Æneas, but shedding no tears over his own death in not loving You, O God" (*Confessions*, bk. 1, chap. 13).

When he was a teenager, Augustine developed a deep friendship with a boy his own age. It was their joy to be together, to exchange ideas, to taste the sweet joys of friendship "sweet to me above all the sweetness of that my life" (*Confessions*, bk. 4, chap. 4). Radiant and charismatic as he was, Augustine exercised a powerful influence on his friend and "from the true faith I had turned him aside" (ibid.).

Suddenly his friend became very ill and, while unconscious, was baptized. Unexpectedly, he recovered. In the course of one of their interchanges, Augustine made fun of what had been done to him while unconscious. To his amazement, his friend, far from agreeing with him, told him that he could not remain his friend if he pursued this course. Augustine was stunned. That was clearly the last thing he expected. Soon afterward, the sickness came back with a vengeance, and the adolescent died.

Referring to this death, Augustine writes that his heart was black with grief. "At this sorrow my heart was utterly darkened, and whatever I looked upon was death" (ibid.). He tasted the bitterness of despair. After a while his pain was assuaged. Reflecting upon this episode, Augustine wrote later: "O madness, which does not know how to love men as men should be loved!" (*Confessions*, bk. 4, chap. 7). "Miserable I was, and miserable is every soul fettered by friendship of perishable things" (ibid.). In times of crisis, man faces a crossroads. When grieving, one possible response is stoicism. "Harden up," nothing is worthy of your tears. Learn to be a man who is above emotions, a "macho" who is too great to be affected by anything.

Augustine was too noble and too generous a son to accept this poisonous solution. But it is true that—shortly after his conversion—he was, for a while, convinced that man's exclusive concern should be God and the salvation of his soul. The rest should be instrumental to achieve this ultimate goal. But as his spiritual and religious life deepened, and upon meditating upon the words of Christ, "Love one another as I have loved you," he realized that the fault he had committed when an adolescent was not that he had loved, but that he had loved wrongly. His friend had become his god. To love a human being more than God simply means to poison his love for his friend. We should love more what is greater; less what is lesser; equally what is equal; unequally what is unequal. But once our heart is truly given to God, in some admirable way we become capable of loving creatures as creatures should be loved.

It is at this point that Augustine develops his profound

philosophical contribution to human love. Creatures should be loved, but they should be loved *in Deo*. It means that the best way of loving creatures is to partake of Christ's love for them. This is perfect love because it is purified love, it is true love. "How could we love more than God those we love in Him?" Augustine exclaims. The tears he had shed over his friend were not illegitimate, because death calls for tears. But they were impure tears or, to put it in Christian language, they were "unbaptized" tears.

The warmhearted Augustine was to shed more tears in his life, but these tears were to be to God's glory. They were the fruits of his contrition, of his gratitude, of his love. Ezekiel begs God to change our hearts of stone into hearts of flesh: hearts that love has made vulnerable. We can assume that Augustine prayed for this grace, and it was granted to him.

In book 8 of the *Confessions* we find some of the greatest lines ever written by a Christian. It etches dramatically the split affecting man's soul since original sin. Augustine had freely chosen to be enslaved by his lust. Now, while seeing clearly that his free will was chained by his vice, he tried desperately to liberate himself—but, "not yet; tomorrow." He willed, but not fully and completely. Moreover, he knew that his bad habits would defeat him, as so often happened when he had tried to cut the chain that bound him to the flesh. Then grace intervenes. How poignant are the lines in which he describes his agony. Victory came through God, and Augustine experienced the inebriating joy of being defeated by Him: this is man's greatest victory.

Contrition, recognition of his sinfulness and helplessness, the voice of the Hound of Heaven pursuing him:
Augustine broke into tears. Opening the Bible, his eyes—
guided by the Holy Spirit—fell on the words of St. Paul
challenging us to leave sin and impurity and "to put on our
Lord Jesus Christ." Exhausted but victorious, Augustine
felt that his chains had fallen away from him. Truth had
made him free. We know the rest of the story. These were
holy tears, purifying tears.

But this great saint, whose heart was as warm as his
intelligence was deep, had to shed more tears. They refer
to his saintly mother's death. She had suffered in bringing
Augustine into the world. But she was to suffer much more
in witnessing the abyss into which he had fallen. She cried,
she begged God for help, she suffered. Monica's ardent love
for her son was shown by her daring even to "pester" a
bishop in Africa by her supplications and constant begging
for his help. Slightly irritated by her insistence, he told her
that "the son of so many tears could not be lost" (*Confessions*, bk. 3, chap. 12).

In His own time, God heard her cries. Augustine was
baptized. In fact, Monica received more than she had asked
for. Augustine decided to lead a celibate life. He would
not do things halfway. She was hoping to have legitimate
grandchildren (for he had a son from his concubine). She
did not know that he would be—and continues to be—a
father to innumerable souls who gratefully drink at the
fountain of his wisdom.

Monica's life was fulfilled. On their way to Africa, they
had to wait in Ostia for the ship taking them back to their

homeland. Mother and son were alone, speaking about eternity, and then—without their asking—they received together a mystical grace that made them taste together the joys of eternity. Monica was about to receive the reward of her faith, her undying hope, her love. She was ripe for eternity. Soon afterward she was taken ill, and soon died. Her last request was that her son would remember her at the altar of the Lord.

Augustine writes: "I closed her eyes and mighty sorrow welled up from the depths of my heart and overflowed in tears" (*Confessions*, bk. 9, chap. 12). Recalling the sweetness of the bond that had linked mother and son, Augustine felt as if his "life was ripped asunder. For out of her life and mine one life had been made" (ibid.). He suffered and wept, but his weeping was before God, "not the tears of a mere man, who would interpret with scorn my weeping" (ibid.).

He continues moving testimony by writing: "If he finds a sin in it that I wept for my mother for a smart part of an hour, for that mother now dead to my eyes who for so many years had wept for me so that I might live in your eyes, let him not laugh me to scorn. But if he is a man of large charity, let him weep over my sins, before the Father of all brothers of your Christ" (ibid.).

Death calls for tears as Virgil wrote: "*Sunt lacrymae rerum.*" But what a difference between the tears the young Augustine shed in his hometown and the pious tears that he shed in Ostia. Taking giant steps after his conversion, Augustine had, through God's grace, learned to shed "baptized tears"—tears of grief, of love, of gratitude that, far from removing us from God, bring us closer to Him—He whose beloved Son was a Man of Sorrow—tears that water the dry soil of our souls and make it blossom into flowers of tenderness and charity.

Holy Mother Church, being a true Mother, knows all the trials that her children have to endure in this vale of tears. For each one she offers a divine remedy that brings solace to the afflicted. She knows how difficult it is for fallen man to shed holy tears and, in her unending love, offers them a prayer (apparently totally forgotten today) begging for the gift of tears. This prayer shows how much she values holy affectivity.

It reads thus:

> Almighty and most gentle God, who didst cause a fountain of living water to gush from the rock in order to quench the thirst of thy people; draw from our hardened hearts tears of compunction, that we may be able to mourn for our sins and merit their forgiveness from thy mercy.
>
> Mercifully regard, O Lord God, the offerings which we make to thy majesty for our sins, and draw from our eyes a flood of tears with which to quench the burning flames which we deserve.

May God grant us the gift of tears, for our Savior said: "Blessed are those that mourn."

HANGING ON CHRIST'S NECK

Previously Unpublished[1]

When I was being prepared for my First Communion, the nun read to us a story relating what had recently taken place in the outskirts of Paris and had been printed in a local church bulletin.

A priest was teaching catechism to deprived children living in the slums of this great city. He was relating with emotion that Christ had been betrayed by one of the twelve apostles whom He called His friends, and that this traitor betrayed Him with a kiss. The latter was rewarded for this abominable deed with thirty pieces of silver, as had been prophesied in the scriptures. Upon hearing that Christ had been condemned to death, Judas went back to the high priests, threw the money in the temple, and hanged himself on a tree.

The children were stunned and remained speechless with horror and, for a while, there was a deadly silence

1. From an unpublished manuscript by Alice von Hildebrand called *Truth and Its Counterfeits.*

in the room. Then all of a sudden, a small boy, aged six, raised his hand and said to the priest: "Father, why didn't Judas hang himself on Christ's neck?"

This story made such an impression on me that, after very many years, I remember it as if I had heard it yesterday. Not only did I not forget it, but thanks to it, I learned a very deep truth, for wisdom can come from the mouth of little children. Up to this day, I remain in the debt of this unknown little chap from the slums of Paris. He taught me that in human life we ultimately have two choices and only two: in despair and self-hatred, to hang ourselves on a tree, and take a life that—given to us by God as an unfathomable gift—has now become unbearable; or to hang ourselves on Christ's neck with deep repentance and immense confidence in His forgiving love.

In both cases, we speak about "hanging." But in the first case, we find self-hatred, self-disgust, sometimes even the craving for self-destruction, and the deep-set conviction that one is beyond redemption. For suicide is the ultimate burial of hope. "There might be hope for someone else, but none for me," such a person is likely to reason; it is just as well that "that remembrance of [me] would be completely obliterated, that there would be no trace of [me]."[2] (This sentence is taken from Kierkegaard, when at the age of twenty-two he was threatened by despair.)

To hang oneself on Christ's neck is the ultimate gesture of confident love. What a gift to know that one can trust in the forgiving love and generosity of a person, because

2. Quoted by Walter Lowrie in his book *A Short Life of Kierkegaard* (Princeton, NJ: Princeton University Press, 2013), 67.

this person is worthy of trust and infinitely good and can not only forgive sins but erase them. Had Judas trusted in Christ's infinite mercy (and he had been granted many opportunities to witness this divine quality during the three privileged years he spent at Christ's side), had he gone back to his master, and "hanged" himself on his neck, crying his eyes out, as Peter did after his denial, this act of confidence and repentance would have saved him. Alas, he chose to mistrust his infinitely good master and opted for perdition.

A person motivated by trust says: "I know that I am deadly ill, sick unto death, but I also know that you are all-loving, all-merciful, all-powerful, and you need only say a word and my soul will be healed. I know that you will never allow that someone who turns to you in confidence, repentance, and humility will be rejected."

Our faith assures us that Christ would have taken the repentant Judas to his heart, erased the deadly kiss of treason with a saving kiss of love, for the divine heart is always moved by contrition and repentance. As it says in Psalm 50:19: "A sacrifice to God is an afflicted spirit: a contrite and humbled heart, O God, thou wilt not despise."

We should all pray: "Help me, O Lord, lest I perish." To deny that man is worth saving, and that Christ can save him, is to hold in contempt His sacrifice on Calvary.

HAVE YOU FORGOTTEN THE SACRAMENTALS?

———

The Wanderer
September 30, 2004

Someone close to me, noticing that I was wearing a scapular, exclaimed with a mixture of pity and contempt, "I did not know that you were superstitious." This grieved me deeply: even though she was raised before Vatican II, she has been so influenced by the spirit of the time that, following the current fashion, she has discarded many of the holy customs of the Holy Church.

Today, young converts have little chance of ever hearing the word "sacramental" while taking religious instructions. A friend of mine, a recent convert, expressed surprise when I happened to mention the word. I explained to her that Holy Church, in her loving care for our souls, puts all sorts of means at our disposal to fight daily temptations and achieve victory over the Evil One.

My friend knew about the seven sacraments, but she

had no idea that throughout the day our Mother offers us means of overcoming the stumbling blocks that we all encounter daily. Whereas the seven sacraments have been instituted by Christ, sacramentals, which like sacraments are exterior signs, have been instituted by the Church. Their reverent use draws upon us God's grace and protects us from dangers. But while the sacraments do produce grace *ex opere operato*, this is not the case with sacramentals. They only help us to obtain it; their efficacy depends upon the disposition of those who use them and comes from the blessing given by the Church to some objects and from the reverent attitude of those using them.

The Bible tells us that the good man falls seven times a day. What should be said of us?

All Catholic homes should have holy water—it is a powerful help to overcome anger, irritation, impatience, temptations, and evil thoughts. The Devil hates it, and St. Teresa of Avila used it frequently to put him to flight. Needless to say, it is to be traced back to Judaism: the Jews were told to purify themselves with water before entering the Temple. Not only is it a powerful means against the attacks of the Evil One, but, moreover, it purifies us of our venial faults when we are truly contrite and repentant.

Blessed incense is also a sacramental. It is used in solemn services, not only to honor the faithful but mainly to purify them.

Blessed candles are lit during severe storms, and placed in the hands of the dying. The day of their blessing is February 2.

The palms blessed on Palm Sunday are endowed with the same virtue. They should be kept in every Catholic home.

The ashes placed on the foreheads of the faithful on Ash Wednesday enjoy the same privilege.

The "Confiteor" is recited at the beginning of Mass (in the Tridentine liturgy it is first recited by the priest and then by the faithful) as a means of purification. It also used to be repeated before receiving Holy Communion. The blessings given by bishops and priests are also a sacramental. Crucifixes, medals, and scapulars also grant us the same help.

It is sad indeed that millions of Catholics today are no longer aware of the privileges that their faith grants them. How many temptations could be overcome, how many evil thoughts could be banished if they only knew that their Mother—the Church—has put all these means at their disposal?

May parish priests once again teach the faithful that divine help is always available to those willing to accept it, and all they need do is gratefully avail themselves of it. The Evil One, like a roaring lion, is always seeking for prey to devour. This truth, alas, is forgotten today.

AN AUDIENCE WITH
JOHN PAUL II

~~~

Crisis Magazine
May 2005

In 1980, I was granted the extraordinary privilege of a private audience with His Holiness Pope John Paul II. Knowing that John Paul had a great admiration for my late husband, I dared make the request. It was granted so fast, I could hardly believe it.

I'd been spending my sabbatical leave in Switzerland and His Holiness had just proclaimed that the fashionable theologian Hans Küng was not a Catholic theologian. Swiss television—Fr. Küng is Swiss—had a field day. Words like "inquisition," "retrograde," and "pre-Vatican II spirit" were repeated *ad nauseam*. Personally, I was deeply grateful for this act of courage; these days, one needs much of this virtue to condemn heresies and errors. The ears of modern men are so often itching.

As soon as the date of the audience was confirmed, I

started thinking seriously about what I was going to say to His Holiness. It seemed to me that first I should express my gratitude for his having warned the sheep of Küng's dangerous ideas. No doubt, the dissident priest was doing a lot of harm, and many of his hearers swallowed his ideas with gusto.

I took the train down to Rome, and, with a beating heart, I was at the bronze door early the next morning. Truth to tell, I was awed and overwhelmed. Soon I would be face to face with the successor of Peter—the representative of Christ on earth, the world's most important human being, for his authority comes directly from God Himself.

Dressed in black, a veil covering my head, I waited in one of the magnificent rooms of the pontifical palace. As I steadied my nerves with prayer, one of the papal dignitaries told me, "The pope is expecting you." I was taken into a huge room where there was a desk and two chairs. The papal chamber attendant introduced me, "Your Holiness, this is Mrs. Dietrich von Hildebrand."

The pope invited me to sit down and then said, "What is on your mind?" I expressed my gratitude for his generosity in receiving me, and for having made the Catholic public aware of the errors Küng was spreading. Coming from Switzerland, I told His Holiness that this act of courage would trigger slanders and persecutions. He expected it, repeating the words of St. Simeon: "The thoughts of many hearts may be revealed."

I also dared to mention that it was regrettable that in

Catholic seminaries some very great thinkers—Augustine, Anselm, Bonaventure—were relatively little known. His Holiness listened carefully and seemed to express his approval.

The thing that struck me most was his *presence*. I truly had the impression that this man—who carried the whole burden of the Church on his shoulders—was giving me his full attention and could have repeated back my every word. He was *fully there*, as if my modest message mattered to him.

My main concern, however, was the fact that the Tridentine Mass had been prohibited. Indeed, some bishops declared that if a person attended the so-called Old Mass on Sunday, he would not thereby fulfill his Sunday obligations. I introduced the question as follows: "Your Holiness, in the last years of his life, my husband was much concerned about an ethical question, namely, whether it is ever legitimate to prohibit a holy tradition. Should not formal prohibitions be limited to what is evil or harmful? The Tridentine Mass has been a precious heritage for centuries, said by all priests until a few years ago. One thing was to introduce a new, valid liturgy, quite another was to prohibit one that all the fathers of Vatican II had prayed during the council." The pope was silent for a brief moment, and then said, "Your husband is no doubt one of the very great ethical thinkers of the twentieth century." I knew that the pope would consider this seriously. Soon afterward he gave the indult.

John Paul II led the Church for almost twenty-seven

years, during one of the most tumultuous periods of her history. There is so much to say about his reign that it might be wiser to wait in order to give a just and thorough assessment of his pontificate. But one thing is certain. He will go down in history as a holy knight.

CHRISTIANS AND THE WORLD

⁓

Catholic News Agency
April 16, 2012

God has given human beings the amazing privilege of speech. Animals communicate by means of sounds and smells, but they have been denied the use of words, that is, meaningful, articulated sounds. This privilege has its own dangers. The riches of the universe, the incredible variety of experiences, feelings, and sensations by far surpasses the human vocabulary as large as it is. This is so true that when referring to experiences that are particularly deep and sublime, we usually say, "Words fail me." Great music does better! We often wish our vocabulary would be as rich as the sublime notes we find in Bach, Haydn, Mozart, Beethoven, and Schubert, to mention but a few.

Moreover, we often use the same word to refer to experiences that are radically different: the word "shame" (in English) refers to things that should make us blush or to things that are mysterious, personal, sacred, sublime, and call for veiling. Let me quote Sirach: "For there is a shame that bringeth sin, and there is a shame that bringeth glory and grace" (Sirach 4:25).

The word "pride" in English refers both to a most poisonous vice and also a compliment: "I am proud of you." In French, pride (*orgueil*) is a negative. We should carefully check the meaning given to words. Failure to do so can lead to grave equivocations. The word "world" is a case in point.

What can we mean by "world"? First, we can refer to the magnificent material universe created by God, with its awesome beauty, embracing immense planets and tiny insects. When creation was completed God declared that it was very good (Genesis 1:31). Great poets have eloquently proclaimed the beauty of the "world." The psalms keep singing God's glory as revealed in nature: "Praise the Lord from the earth, ye dragons, and all ye deeps: fire, hail, snow, ice, stormy winds which fulfill his word" (Psalm 148:7–8).

When God called His creation "good," He was referring to its ontological dignity and not to any moral quality. Only personal beings can be "morally good" or "morally evil." This clarification is crucial. There is not a single being coming out of the Creator's hands that is deprived of ontological value and, therefore, is not "good." But there are many who erroneously assume that this also applies to human actions, and that, therefore, everything being good, what we call evil is only a lack of goodness, and that it is a duty of charity to look for the good behind the evil. Moral disvalues entered the world through sin.

Let us compare this praise of the "world" with the

words that Christ used at the Last Supper as related by St. John. He tells us that the world "does not know my Father." This chapter, containing the most sublime words ever uttered by the God-Man, is also the one proclaiming the most fearful condemnation of "the world," found in John 17:9: "I pray not for the world." He, who is Love incarnate (there is no greater love than to offer one's life for one's friends), utters a conviction of the "world" that is so fearful that every time I read it I shudder. Christ goes further. He tells us that the "world" hates Him—the Holy One—and tells His disciples that just as the "world" has hated Him, it will hate them too because they loved Him.

What does He mean by these fearful words? Other passages of the Gospel give us a clue. When referring to the "world," Christ clearly means the Kingdom of Satan, the Prince of this World, a murderer from the very beginning, the incarnate lie, and the archenemy of the one who said, "I am the Truth." It is therefore luminous why He refuses to pray for a world that is Lucifer's kingdom. One cannot save whoever has solemnly rejected salvation. How right C. S. Lewis was when he wrote that the doors of hell are locked from the inside. Because they do not want redemption, they hate the Redeemer.

In his monumental work *The Liturgical Year*, Dom Gueranger writes, "The fundamental rule of Christian life is, as almost every page of the Gospel tells us, that we should live out of the world, separate ourselves from the world, hate the world. The world is that ungodly land which Abraham, our sublime model, is commanded by God to quit. It is that Babylon of our exile and captivity, where we are beset with dangers. The beloved disciple cries out to us, 'Love not the world, nor the things which are in the world. If any man loves the world, the charity of the Father is not in him.'"

These words are fearful indeed. Those of us still in this vale of tears should never lose sight of the fact that we are in a battlefield facing the Enemy of mankind who, like a roaring lion, looks for a victim to devour. A moment of somnolence, a moment of self-assurance, can bring about a grave moral fall. It can even happen when administering an exorcism, that is, in a face to face confrontation with the Evil One, when armed with the powerful tools given us by Holy Church.

Our deadly enemy never sleeps. He can tempt monks fleeing into the desert (St. Anthony); he can penetrate religious orders; he can prey on us while in Church. *Sobrii estote et vigilate* (Be sober and vigilant).

But the message of Christ is luminous: the world in this sense is the Kingdom of Evil. There is a clear choice: either the City of God or the City of Satan. There is no "both/and," there is no "in between," just as there is little middle ground between the truth and a lie. The "world" as the City of Satan is our deadly enemy.

Finally, we can mean by "world" the society in which we are born and in which we live. (Very few of us receive the extraordinary vocation to be anchorites.) But those blessed with spiritual hearing not only believe but know that silence, contemplation, prayer, and penance do more for the world than "busyness" can ever achieve. It is often self-seeking, garbed with the vestment of "love for humanity." Behind this façade lurks the pursuit of honor, money, and power. It is noisy, but does not create music.

Most of us are called to live in society with other human beings coming from a huge variety of backgrounds, cultures, and beliefs. If one lives in an apartment building, one is inevitably in daily contact with a surprising variety of views and outlooks. Some people are believers; some are indifferent; some are atheists. Some are kind and helpful. Some are unfriendly and selfish. A single such building is a "small cosmos," and could be an inspiration for any talented writer.

This also applies to one's professional life. Spending one's life teaching at a university is a most enriching experience. It is true indeed that one finds both "wheat" and "cockle" wherever we go. It is, however, seriously misleading to write that this also applies to the Church and to the world without making it clear that by "church" is meant the sinful members of the church and not the Church as Holy Bride of Christ who is "without blemish and without wrinkles." I know by experience that non-Catholics have no idea what is meant by the Holy Catholic Church. It is true that the fields of both the "church" and the world share the same fate: a mixture of good and evil. But the consequence to be drawn is that we should wisely pick up the wheat in both fields while rejecting the tares they share.

This claim sounds charitable and fair. To state that we find "weeds" in the "church" (its members) is sadly true, provided it clearly refers to its sinners who "officially" belong to the Church. Among her members, there are good and bad fish. The Bible tells us that although the Jews were God's chosen ones, and therefore highly privileged people, there were good and holy ones, and also great sinners.

This also applies to the "pagan" world. It gave us a Socrates and some very unsavory characters. When Socrates declared that if someone proved him to be wrong, he would consider him to be his greatest benefactor, our response should be one of boundless admiration. It is a superb "existential" refutation of the Calvinistic claim that original sin has perverted our nature to its very core. Our modern world would do well to learn from the wise man of Greece (as Kierkegaard always refers to him), and whom Plato called "the wisest and justest (*sic*) and the best man I have ever known."[1] Such wise men are rare and desperately needed today in our colleges and universities.

We cannot "flee" from the world in this sense. If God placed us in a concrete situation, this is where He expects us to place our humble talents at His service. Every Catholic, every Christian for that matter, is necessarily "engaged" in the world and is called upon to be a missionary: we have been the beneficiaries of the Good News and are called upon to share it with others. The radiance of this message of joy can even lead to a conversion in an elevator, as I was once privileged to experience!

But we should not assume that because it is our mission to "engage" in the world, we need not take precautions when entering a "danger zone," and can forget for a single moment that Satan never sleeps.

---

1. *Phaedo* 118.

No man is permitted to practice medicine if he does not have a valid medical diploma. No one can teach at a university if he does not have the proper credentials. If one does not practice his faith, does not pray, forgets that "without God he can do nothing," and thereby "engages" in our so-called culture and our decadent world, he is like a person visiting a patient afflicted by an infectious disease without wearing protective garments.

One cannot give what one does not have. The endemic ignorance of their faith that characterized most Catholics in the aftermath of Vatican II has not equipped them to do "missionary" work. He who has accepted the popular view that everything is relative, and that everyone has a right to his own opinion (why should your opinion be better than mine?) not only cannot help others but, moreover, is likely to catch their disease.

Worse yet are those infected by the spirit of the time, who "believe" that the Church has changed on all fundamental issues, has finally come out of the ghetto of the Middle Ages; such a person is eloquent at propagating heresies, whether he realizes it or not.

There are also those armed with a shallow optimism who assume that everybody is good, or at least seeks the good, and who are totally unaware of the difficulty of evangelization. The danger is great for the evangelizer who goes about his "mission" quite unprepared for the arduous task lying before him, who remains unaware that our society is afflicted with some deadly disease, and who refuses to take the indispensable precautions to protect himself from catching the contagious disease of dictatorial relativism. Before "engaging" with the world, prayer, the sacraments, and sacrifice are essentially required.

Alas, many sicknesses are contagious—health is not. Those of us who have had the doubtful privilege of staying long in rehab, and became acquainted with the layout of these places of penance—my name for hospitals—know that there is a special section for infectious diseases. No one is permitted to enter except those who have received the assignment of serving the sick. But before entering this forbidden space, doctors and nurses cover themselves with special gowns, wear masks, never touch the patient directly, and, upon leaving the room, once again, go through a whole procedure to make sure that they have not caught deadly germs.

Are these precautions taken by those Catholics who "engage with the world" and so expose themselves to grave moral dangers? There are "red zones," including certain types of bars, movies, and dark places where most people should never enter. What of those poor creatures enslaved in such places of harm? Should they be abandoned to their fate? Far from it; we all have the strict duty to pray and sacrifice for those of our brothers who are "sick unto death." Moreover, there are extraordinary cases in which God calls some of His children to penetrate into places of horror because He has given them a special mission. For them it had become their "*thema Christi*" (theme of Christ). St. Raymond of Penafort and St. Peter Nolasco received the mission to go to the dreadful jails in North Africa where innumerable Christians were held captive by the Moors in the most awful moral, physical, and psychological conditions.

They did great work because they were spiritually armed and never forgot that without God they could do nothing. Those called upon to actively "engage" in the world and its decadent culture need a long novitiate. It is easy to harm our neighbor; it is only with God's grace that we can truly help him.

CLASSROOM CONVERSION

National Catholic Register
March 20, 1983

Not long ago, in my "Introduction to Philosophy" course, I was discussing truth. I gave my students the classical argument against subjectivism and relativism, namely, that whenever one tries to deny objective truth, one must simultaneously claim that one's own statement is itself true, really and objectively.

Suddenly, a male student raised his hand, rose (a most unusual occurrence), and said in a strong, clear voice: "I object, Professor, to your spreading Roman Catholicism in this classroom." There followed a moment of great tension, and my thoughts rushed to God for help. Then I said quietly: "I'm afraid that you are guilty of an anachronism." Since the student did not know what I meant, I explained: "The argument I have been using is taken from Plato, who lived some four centuries before the birth of Christ. He can hardly be called a Roman Catholic. This should answer your objection." I then proceeded with my teaching.

Some sixteen months later, I received a phone call just as I was about to leave for the university, where I was scheduled to proctor exams for the evening. The person who was calling, a former student, said she urgently wanted to see me. I told her that this was not possible since I was to be on duty the whole evening, and, furthermore, it was my last day at the university until the fall term. She started to cry and insisted that she had to see me immediately. Surmising that her problem was truly serious, I contacted a friend of mine who agreed to proctor in my stead.

I then rushed to the university. I hardly had time to take off my coat when the girl who had phoned me came in. I immediately recognized her—even though she had never spoken to me personally when she was my student. She had a fine, sensitive face, and I had been impressed by her attentiveness and eagerness to listen. To my utter amazement, she told me abruptly that she wanted to become a Roman Catholic. I was so surprised that I was speechless, but I then decided to test her. "Why?" I asked. "Your courses convinced me." "But," I responded, "I didn't say a word about religion in my classes; my topic is philosophy."

"I know," she answered, "but do you recall an incident about sixteen months ago when a student got up and objected to your refutation of subjectivism and relativism on the grounds that you were spreading Roman Catholicism in the classroom? I had been brought up with strong anti-Catholic prejudices. But just when the student spoke out, the grace of God struck me. I suddenly understood that the Roman Catholic Church *does* stand for the objectivity of truth and that I had been blinded by prejudices."

"Your course helped me very much, and I decided to take another one with you," she continued. "I heard through another student that you were the wife of a famous Roman Catholic writer, Dietrich von Hildebrand. I rushed to the library and read a couple of his works. Now I am convinced. Please, help me to find a good priest so that I can take instructions in the faith."

This is how L. C. found her way into the Church. I learned a great lesson through her experience: God is so powerful, so great, that He can use anything for the good. Obviously the student who had objected to my teaching (a fallen away Catholic, I fear) wanted to hurt me—to "warn" the other students of the danger of taking a course taught by a "bigoted" person. Since many of my students are atheists, the name "Roman Catholic" is taboo. He wanted to say to all his fellow students: "Be on your guard; you are treading on treacherous ground."

Yet such an attitude and such words of warning are what God used to draw someone to Himself. St. Augustine indeed was correct when he wrote that God judged it "more befitting His power and goodness to bring good out of evil than to prevent the evil from coming into existence" (*City of God*, bk. 22, chap. 1).

Indeed, God always has the last word.

AN INTERVIEW WITH
ALICE VON HILDEBRAND

———◆———

America Magazine,
October 22, 2014[1]

If you could tell people one thing about your late husband Dietrich, what would it be?

Coming from a very Catholic background, I had met many deeply committed Catholics in my life—priests, nuns, and lay people (my father being one of them)—but I had never met one who out of love for God, and love for truth and justice, gave up everything in order to fight evil. For the first time in my life, I met a hero. He was not someone who by nature was "macho": he hated fights, dissensions, and so on. But when the call came, he never hesitated.

Remarkably, he did not experience fear when he knew his life was threatened daily. I am ever moved when I read

1. This is a substantial excerpt from an interview with Sean Salai, SJ, that appeared at *America Magazine* online.

the passage in his memoirs after he is warned by the chief of the secret police in Vienna that an assassination order had gone out for him. My husband writes, "Though I am fearful of physical dangers, I was not afraid; I was not intimidated by what he had told me. I had the consciousness that I was conducting a struggle willed by God, and this gave me an incredible inner freedom."

He never lamented all that he had lost, unlike so many other refugees. He went from a mansion in Munich to the slums of New York. Like St. Paul, he could live in riches and in utter poverty. This made such a deep impression upon me that a seed was planted in my heart that played a profound role in awakening my love for him. When I first met him, my overwhelming feeling was awe.

He was called upon to play the role of Cassandra, and so he soon discovered that people hate bad news. Just as they are leading their daily lives, working and trying to "succeed," here comes someone who warns them that they should arm themselves for a deadly fight. I am convinced that today his message would be very much the same.

You and your husband met at Fordham University when you were a graduate student and he was your professor. What made you fall in love with him?

One falls in love with someone when one is granted the privilege of seeing the beauty that God placed in them at the moment of their creation. I call it the "Tabor vision." This vision touches one's heart, and we must always seek to keep it alive, for it is the seal of "faithfulness." I was granted this "Tabor vision" of Dietrich von Hildebrand, and it gives a key to our marriage.

You were both Catholic intellectuals, but with different philosophical perspectives. What was your marriage like?

Neither Dietrich von Hildebrand nor I ever claimed to be theologians—even though he is often called one. Through him I fell in love with "the love of wisdom" and devoted my life to increasing and deepening my knowledge, and then sharing it with thousands of students at Hunter College in the City University of New York. Teaching taught me that souls are starving for truth and mostly deprived of it. I also learned that when truth is freely offered to them many find their way to God. The great enemy of truth is relativism in all its forms, falsely presented as "democracy," as anti-totalitarianism, as rolling back a supposed dark ages. In fact, to embrace relativism is to return to the dark cave from which Plato's philosopher escaped, while to embrace the existence of truth, even when it means the risk of attacks and persecution, is to reenter the cave in order to liberate those who remain trapped in the realm of shadows. Truth is never "mine"; it is always "ours." Truth unites, while error divides.

The deep bond between my husband and me was our common love for the one true Church, for truth, for beauty and moral goodness. We loved anything with a genuine spiritual and cultural *sursum corda*: great classical music, great paintings, great architecture, and great literature.

My husband had a special talent for showing that visible and audible beauty clearly hint at God, who is Beauty itself. We shared the same love for saints and had the same friends. We shared everything important.

What did it mean for you to be named a Grand Dame of the Order of St. Gregory by Pope Francis last year?

I was joyfully conscious when I became Lady Alice that my husband—now in eternity—was the true recipient.

Some people consider you a Christian feminist.
How do you understand feminism?

To distinguish myself clearly from Simone de Beauvoir's powerful and poisonous book, *The Second Sex*, I would not call myself a Christian feminist but a champion of femininity. The sublime beauty of the female mission as virgin, wife, or mother has been so degraded that I felt a calling to shed light on "the privilege of being a woman," which is also the title of one of my books.

Of all creatures mentioned in Genesis, Eve is the only one whose body is taken from the body of a person; even Adam's body was taken from the "slime of the earth." She is declared by Adam to be the "mother of the living." He is not called the "father of the living." When Eve gives birth to Cain, she ecstatically says: I have brought a child into the world with God's help. Adam, the biological father, is not mentioned. Eve proclaims that the child's soul—which is made to God's image and likeness—is placed by God

Himself into her body. God, so to speak, "touches" the female body and in so doing gives it a note of sacredness.

The duel that takes place between the woman and the serpent, not between "the strong sex" and the serpent, hints at the crucial role of women in the economy of redemption. The most perfect of all creatures, queen of the angels, is a woman—not a man. It is high time that women should humbly acknowledge that they are privileged to be women.

What do you hope people will take away from your life and career?

My career, which took place in a deeply antagonistic milieu, taught me that "with God all things are possible" (Matthew 9:26) and that "I can do all things in Him who strengthens me" (Philippians 4:13).

What's your favorite scripture verse and why?

"Unless you become like little children, you shall not enter the kingdom of heaven" (Matthew 18:3). How important it is to meditate on these divine words, particularly in universities where "aristocratic stupidities" (that is, intellectual errors) are so often greeted with respect.

If you could say one thing to Pope Francis, what would it be?

I would greet Pope Francis as the successor of St. Peter, who, like Francis today, was the first to receive the sublime mission of transmitting the divine message—without changing one iota. The Holy Catholic Church has always lived up to this great mission, to hold fast to the golden cord of tradition that stretches all the way back to Christ Himself.

Do you have any final thoughts or hopes for the future?

The future is in God's hands. One cannot err by meditating on the New Testament, where both St. Matthew and St. Luke warn us that, at the end of time—and inevitably we are coming closer—there will be such confusion as to mislead even the elect.

Watch and pray, lest you fall into temptation. May God grant us the gifts of *faith* and *hope* at moments when humanly speaking we have reason to be threatened by despair. "These things I have spoken to you, that in me you may have peace. In the world you shall have distress: but have confidence, I have overcome the world" (John 16:33).

PART II

⟋⟍

REMEMBRANCES OF
ALICE VON HILDEBRAND
BY HER FRIENDS

PERSONAL REMEMBRANCES OF ALICE VON HILDEBRAND

~

Raymond Leo Cardinal Burke

SHRINE OF OUR LADY OF GUADALUPE

Alice von Hildebrand was a person of extraordinary intellect and cultural refinement, who, at the same time, had a child-like faith, in the highest sense of the word. It was clear that she lived daily an intense relationship with Our Lord in the Church. The depth of her philosophical and theological knowledge found its consummation in an intense life of faith. She came from a distinguished, faithfully Catholic family in French-speaking Belgium. She faithfully handed on to others the faith which was handed on to her in her family and in the wider Church. Of course, meeting Dietrich von Hildebrand and eventually entering into Holy Matrimony with him was the greatest gift—after family, life and the Faith—which Our Lord gave to her.

She was always in spiritual communion with her beloved husband whom Our Lord called to Himself in 1977. In my visits with her during her last years, she spoke frequently of how she longed to go to Our Lord and thus to be once again with her dearly loved Dietrich. It was a great blessing to have met her and to enjoy her friendship which was deeply loyal.

Rocco Buttiglione

ITALIAN PHILOSOPHER AND STATESMAN

Her appearance was very feminine and fragile, but she was never afraid. She had the heart of a lioness and was very conscious of the privilege of womanhood. Men are easily tempted to put their confidence in themselves and in their own strength. She always put her confidence in the strength of the Lord, and this is the reason why she was never afraid. She was intensely intellectual, but her intelligence was purified by love, the love of God "that moves the sun and the other stars." It is impossible to remember her without remembering her husband. Dietrich von Hildebrand had been to her the human love that leads into the greater love of God, the sacrament, the visible and efficacious sign of the love of God. She felt profoundly the mystery of liturgy that binds together heaven and earth and keeps the Church united. She was always intent on uniting in truth and love. She loved Italy and loved Dante. When I think of her I think of the first line of the sonnet Dante dedicated to Beatrice: "My Lady looks so gentle and so pure...." She really was a "Beatrice": one who leads into the realm of grace, of beauty, and of truth.

Jean Pierre Casey

NEPHEW OF ALICE VON HILDEBRAND

If I had to characterize Aunt Lily's contributions to the Church in one statement, it is that her entire professional life was guided by a relentless pursuit and defense of the truth. Of course, her professional life and her personal life were indistinguishable, to the extent that she made this defense of the Church's perennial teachings her life's mission, and to the extent that fueling her on this quest was her personal love of Christ and regular frequenting of the sacraments. With her characteristic grace, wit, and charm, she was able to disarm her most rabid opponents, without ever making philosophical differences personal. And yet behind the velvet glove lay a will of steel and an incisive mind, which prolifically doled out fierce argumentation. To use Margaret Thatcher's expression, "this lady was not for turning." In an age of doctrinal confusion and militant secularism, the legacy that she and uncle Dietrich—an intellectual monument of a couple—leave behind can be summarized in John 8:32: "The truth shall set you free."

Ronda Chervin

AUTHOR, PROFESSOR OF PHILOSOPHY, AND
STUDENT OF DIETRICH VON HILDEBRAND

I met Alice von Hildebrand in 1957. She has been my role model and mentor ever since. Her wonderful witty way of addressing the questions asked by her students at Hunter

College, who were mostly atheists, helped me become a Catholic. An example: if a student defended abortion based on "the little thing is just a cell," she would say, "Oh, so if your mother is pregnant, she thinks it might be a dog or cat coming in the future!" She would always study with love the souls of all her friends and could come up with succinct but potent answers to questions such as, "In case you leave this earth and I never see you again, what would you advise me about how to grow?" Her answer to me: "You are too active, you need to be much more receptive."

Peter J. Colosi

SALVE REGINA UNIVERSITY

I can remember Alice von Hildebrand from when she would occasionally come to campus at Franciscan University when I was an undergraduate; I recall there was always an air of excitement when she was arriving, a buzz among the students wondering what she would speak about this visit. I got to know her a bit more during the times she would visit the International Academy for Philosophy in Liechtenstein, and then even more over the ensuing years when she would be present at conferences and at friends' houses. I always felt honored that she remembered me and my name, even though our encounters were never very long conversations. I was also always quite struck by her wakefulness, if that's the right word: she was always affectively quite alive whenever she faced a person for a conversation and remained so throughout the conversation, no matter how short or long—it was quite an engaging experience.

In my short but memorable conversations with her over the years, I would also say that she had a type of balance between two "themes." On the one hand, there was a deep interest in the actual topic of the conversation, which manifested itself in a naturally emerging wisdom about any topic, along with references to great thinkers (especially Kierkegaard) in her responses. Then, on the other hand—but "on the other hand" isn't quite the right expression, because this second "theme" also added to the depth of the philosophical discussion—there was a joy and exuberance that naturally drew one into the flow of the encounter; I would describe it as a kind of joyful playfulness, which manifested itself in her way of weaving in anecdotes or little "jokes" along the way, which always pertained somehow to the philosophical topic at hand, oftentimes helping to deepen the grasp of a philosophical point: at the very same time that this second "theme" lightened the conversation, it also somehow deepened it. In these encounters one always had the sense that she was interested in you as a person and not only in the topic of the discussion.

John Henry Crosby

HILDEBRAND PROJECT

Since Lily von Hildebrand's passing, I have been sent back "into the caverns of memory," as she would often say, as recollections of our nearly twenty years of close collaboration come back to me. We were, in some ways, an unlikely duo when we launched the Hildebrand Project in 2004: she, venerable, brilliant, and prolific, and I, just twenty-five, untried and in search of my life's work. I first discovered her unique genius around 1994 when I was sixteen. I had the great privilege of being invited to her New Rochelle apartment for a tête-à-tête, as she was fond of describing conversations with friends. I remember feeling that I'd never before met someone with such charm, wisdom, and zest for life. For nearly twelve years, until she became homebound, we took innumerable trips together in service of the Hildebrand Project. One of the most unforgettable was our journey to Rome in 2007. We had the tremendous privilege of meeting Pope Benedict XVI in private audience—a sign of the Holy Father's deep regard not just for her late, great husband but also for herself. She was visibly moved to be meeting the Vicar of Christ on earth. I was moved by her trembling heart, and this was a great gift to me, as through her eyes—I saw and felt—the awesome reality of Peter among us, more deeply than I could have on my own. Even in her high nineties, she never lost the ability to be deeply moved by all that is good, true, and beautiful. She was uniquely invested in the lives of those she loved; sometimes I had the feeling she had greater joy in our joys and deeper sorrow at our sorrows than we ourselves. This is surely why so many of us opened our hearts to Lily. She received us as we were and accompanied us with tender love. I never doubted that she would fulfill her pledge of prayers for me. This full engagement of her heart also gave her faith a unique and convincing power that will ever remain with me. Whatever doubts or difficulties she may have experienced, these could not compare with the depth of her faith in Jesus and His promises. The gravestone she now shares with her beloved husband Dietrich could not capture this more perfectly: "Lord, you know that I love you" (John 21:15).

William Doino Jr.

HISTORIAN

I first encountered Lily von Hildebrand in the 1980s, during one of her famous talks critiquing relativism. Her voice was as soft as a whisper, but it carried the power of a mighty battleship. As gifted a speaker as she was, however, there was nothing like meeting her in person. Lily had the unique ability to make her acquaintances appreciate the grandeur and beauty of life—while inspiring them to love and serve God ever more faithfully, in response to this precious gift.

I knew Lily for almost thirty years, and was close friends with her the last twenty of her life. She frequently and gratefully drew upon the profound insights of her legendary husband, Dietrich, but she was a dazzling thinker in her own right. Her rich and overflowing wisdom left an indelible impression on my soul. Not a minute I spent with her was wasted. The biggest lessons I learned from Lily were the importance of truth, humility, reverence and above all, one's eternal salvation. I can't remember a time I spoke to her when all four beliefs were not, in some way, conveyed in an unmistakable manner.

I've never had a greater friend, never had a greater teacher, and never met a lay person who better exemplified what it means to be a Christian in the contemporary world. May Lily von Hildebrand's legacy grow, and may it continue to point people toward Heaven!

Anthony Esolen

WORD AND SONG

Rest in peace, my friend Dr. Alice von Hildebrand (1923–2022).

I first met Lily at the rectory of Saint John the Evangelist, in Stamford, Connecticut. I had been invited by our mutual friend Fr. Paul Check to give a talk to some 150 parishioners on Shakespeare, so I spoke about purity in *The Tempest*. I chose the topic advisedly, because I'd read Dietrich von Hildebrand's treatise on purity, *Reinheit und Jungfräulichkeit*, and I knew that young people needed to be inspired by the beauty of an ideal, and not merely given a set of moral prohibitions.

But before the talk, Fr. Check and I had dinner with a few other priests and with his friend and a frequent guest, Alice von Hildebrand, Dietrich's widow. When she first arrived, I went up to her and said, "Professor, I am honored to meet you." She shook my hand and said, with a twinkle in her eye, "And who are you?" We hit it off immediately, and tremendously. All through supper we talked about literature—not philosophy. I doubt that many trained philosophers in our time could have held their own with her in the conversation. It seems that her beloved husband Dietrich was a lover of Cervantes, and that he would read *Don Quixote* once every year. So they were in Mexico once, early in their marriage, and he asked her to read *Don Quixote* to him.

"But I can't really read Spanish," she said.

"That's all right," said he. "I know what it means already anyway."

It's quite appropriate that they should be enthralled by Cervantes, the brave soldier who lost the use of his left arm at the Battle of Lepanto, and who was so daring and noble, he won the affection of his Moorish captors when he was a prisoner of war four years later. For, as early as 1921—consider that date very carefully—Dietrich von Hildebrand inveighed against the stupidity of racialism, anti-Judaism, and Nazism. For much of the 1930s, official cutting-edge liberal eugenicist America was playing footsie with Hitler, but Hildebrand saw into him and through him from the first, and was a vocal and relentless foe, much to the cost of his career and his worldly prospects. After the putsch in Austria and the assassination of the much maligned and still slandered Catholic chancellor, Engelbert Dollfuss, Dietrich von Hildebrand and his wife—Lily married him much later, when he was a widower—escaped from Austria on the last train out, with Swiss passports. He was tops on Hitler's list of men to be obliterated.

Lily was utterly devoted to her husband's intellectual work, which is immense, and most of it is still not available in English. And she was a powerful thinker in her own right, a formidable woman. We met quite a few times after that meeting, and we corresponded, too. For the last ten years, she has been in a good deal of physical discomfort and pain. She told me that she put stoups of holy water here and there through her house, to help her practice what she called "holy pestering," that is, petitions to God to alleviate her suffering by taking her away, yet not her will but His was to be done.

It is strange to consider that everyone who knew Lily was only three degrees of separation from Edmund Husserl, who was Dietrich's teacher and mentor, Edith Stein and others in that intellectual crowd, Max Scheler, the conductor Wilhelm Furtwängler, Dietrich's father the monumental sculptor Adolf von Hildebrand—and Hitler. Yet Dietrich's native language was not German, but Italian; he spent his boyhood in Tuscany. When he lay dying, as Lily has written in her beautiful biography, *Soul of a Lion*, he could no longer speak German or English or French or Spanish, but only Italian.

Lily von Hildebrand was a good and brave and gracious woman, whose breadth and depth of reading would make most professors in our time look like rather clever but ill-bred and ill-read high schoolers.

Requiem aeternam dona ei, Domine, et lux perpetua luceat super eam.

Maria Fedoryka

AVE MARIA UNIVERSITY

My best memories of Lily are from the end of her life. Despite her countless physical ailments, and the breakdown of the body that often comes with old age, she seemed to become loving in an entirely new way. I never once heard her complain about her bodily suffering (which has left a deep impression on me), and I have imagined that the acceptance of her suffering carved out a new chamber in her heart, which she had prepared for all her life, and which now came to fruition. The last time my husband saw her was just ten days before her death—and she was still full of two things so characteristic of her: a boundless enthusiasm for talking about the truth, and humor!

Dana Gioia

POET AND FORMER CHAIRMAN OF THE
NATIONAL ENDOWMENT FOR THE ARTS

I was the Chairman of the National Endowment for the Arts when I first encountered the formidable Alice von Hildebrand. I had recently met with John Henry Crosby about his notion of translating Dietrich von Hildebrand's *Aesthetics* into English. It was a project that both of us knew was significant. I asked him to prepare a formal description of his idea for a possible Chairman's grant.

On our second meeting I was slightly surprised that he

brought along the philosopher's widow. Into my over-large, high-ceilinged office in the Old Post Office came a small and elegant, elderly woman. We sat down at the conference table, and she began gently but tenaciously to cross-examine me. John Henry might think I was okay, but she wasn't so sure. I needed to be vetted. Lily quizzed me on my background, education, worldview, and aesthetics. I realized that I was getting a job interview: Was I worthy of funding her late husband's legacy?

Finally, Lily looked me in the eye and asked who was the greatest poet who ever lived. I told her that it was impossible to select a single writer when literature was a human enterprise of continuous, diverse, and distinct achievement, full of irreplaceable high points. Even within the Western tradition there was no reasonable way to pick a single writer as preeminent.

She was sweet but unrelenting. But who would you pick, she replied, if you could pick only one? I told her I could only judge poets whose work I could read in the original languages. I could not judge Pushkin or Homer's greatness. Then judge from the five languages you know, she urged. I gave her half a dozen poets of sublime stature—Virgil, Horace, Dante, Shakespeare, Goethe, Milton, Baudelaire. But which, she insisted, would you pick as the greatest poet of the Western tradition? She would not be appeased without an answer, so I told her it would have to be Dante Alighieri.

"That is the right answer," she declared. Having passed the exam, I was allowed to begin our meeting.

Alice Ann Grayson

VEIL OF INNOCENCE

I founded Veil of Innocence under the direct personal influence of Alice von Hildebrand, known affectionately as "Lily." Lily was indeed the perfect nickname for this woman who devoted her life to forming her many followers to love the virtue of purity in all states of life: single, consecrated celibacy, and holy marriage. Lily served on the board of directors of Veil of Innocence for twenty-one years.

I grew so close to Lily that I would call her my adopted mother, and she thought of me as her adopted daughter. We laughed as she aged that our roles were reversing, and I would be looking out for her needs, rather than the other way around. In her later years, each time my husband and I visited Lily, she would repeatedly say, "Friendship is the remnant of paradise." Her joy was being close to her friends and sharing in their lives. She lived through us.

Lily's sudden passing caught us by surprise, even though she was 98! She started to sleep more and more. A kindly priest visited her and celebrated Holy Mass and anointed her. Although I was not able to be with Lily at the time of her death, I was able to call the nurse's cell phone and asked her to put the phone next to her ear. I told Lily that I was coming the next day, but it was alright if God wanted her sooner.

Scott Hahn

ST. PAUL CENTER FOR BIBLICAL THEOLOGY

I will miss Alice von Hildebrand the way I would miss gravity if it were taken away. Lily was a quiet force, a presence, an authority, a constant in my professional and cultural world. She was a true sage and a true friend, brilliant, but utterly without pretense. She spoke with the clarity of nature as it produces mountains. I grieve for the loss of her, and I would grieve more if she had not spent a long life influencing so many people in the world I shared with her—the world where you and I live on.

James A. Harold

FRANCISCAN UNIVERSITY OF STEUBENVILLE

I did not know Mrs. von Hildebrand as "Lily," with all the familiarity that a first-name basis implies. She was always to me "Mrs. von Hildebrand." I could see, even from a distance, how both clear and deep she was as a thinker and lecturer. Furthermore, what struck me about Mrs. von Hildebrand was her particular exemplification of the description, *coincidencia oppositorum*. Philosophers note that the higher the kind of being is, the more that being can contain seeming opposites. Applying this idea to Mrs. von Hildebrand, she was, on the one hand, feminine, in the best sense of the word: sweet, kind, gracious. On the other hand, there was something of a lioness in her. Odd, she was obviously not physically imposing. Her power all went back to faithful goodness, intelligence, and strength of character. That strength came in handy when she teamed up with Fr. Benedict Groeschel, C.F.R., while both were serving on the Franciscan University Board of Trustees, to pick a new university president. Apparently, there were some battles, and the wisdom, strength, and goodness of this holy woman and priest were decisively important for the university. Thank you, Mrs. von Hildebrand.

Michael Healy

FRANCISCAN UNIVERSITY OF STEUBENVILLE

I first encountered Alice von Hildebrand over fifty years ago as an undergraduate at Loyola University of Los Angeles. She was there to give a talk on how Søren Kierkegaard dealt with the theological liberals of his day (the nineteenth century). Her address was filled with tremendous insight as well as humor. Over time I discovered that this combination was deeply characteristic of her entire life and thought! Her lecture became a life-changing experience for me and set me on the road to a rediscovery of Catholic faith and tradition. Now, at seventy-one, after slogging clumsily and imperfectly through many decades of attempting to live the devout life at home (marriage, five kids) and at work (teaching and administrating), I was again touched by her spirit and renewed in hope—looking back on my own struggles and failures—after reading one of her final books of wisdom, *Memoirs of a Happy Failure*. Marvelous! God bless you, Lily, and thank you!

Doug Keck

PRESIDENT, EWTN

Our great friend Lily was truly one-of-a-kind! Over the years we got to be good friends and she was very kind to me and my entire family for which we will forever be grateful. The first time I got to work with Lily was in 1997, when she did a program for EWTN called "Feminism or Femininity." While she was down here teaching and doing the program I had a chance to do my first couple of book interviews with her for the *Bookmark* show. Back then we took a promo break halfway through the show. Just before we began, I mentioned to her that when we had to go to the break I would gently tap her foot to let her know to wrap up her comment. She gave her typical knowing nod and we began the interview. Halfway through the program as we approached the break I tapped her on her shoe as I had indicated I would. She responded immediately exclaiming "Mr. Keck, why are you kicking me?!" I will forever remember that moment as it was the beginning of a long-distance email friendship that was punctuated with several interviews and programs throughout the years.

Peter Kreeft

BOSTON COLLEGE

My most memorable remembrance of Lily was the time she came to Boston College to talk to about a hundred female students about what it means to be a Catholic woman. They were absolutely stunned. They had never heard her common sense and faithful transmission and defense of the Church's perennial answer to that question before. Clarity and charity—they had heard little of either and never both together. Lily, like her husband, was a gentle but formidable lion—an Aslan!

Robert Kreppel

FRIEND AND FORMER STUDENT

It was back in 1963 when I first met Alice von Hildebrand at Hunter College in New York City. She taught philosophy in the evening and was known to her students as Dr. Jourdain. I was a student and can recall arriving by subway and then taking the elevator to the seventh floor where her classroom would always be popular. Here secular relativism would be challenged and developing minds would be introduced by a brilliant teacher to a world of absolute values. She retired from Hunter College in 1984, and over the years I would see her at speaking events and award dinners. On my birthday she would always remember me during her daily Mass. She continued to be a teacher for us all. Friends would call her Lily. But when speaking or writing to her I would always call her Dr. Jourdain. Remembering her I am so grateful that she came into my life and that I can be part of the Hildebrand Project.

Robert Luddy

FOUNDER AND PRESIDENT, CAPTIVEAIRE

FOUNDER, THALES ACADEMY

The most important lessons Lily von Hildebrand taught were not necessarily the academic lectures she gave her students at Hunter College. There are two lessons she taught to the school of life that have particularly influenced me and those with whom I share her wisdom. For Lily, gratitude was the primary requirement for personal happiness. This was made known not only by her words but through the way she lived. As a Catholic, female philosopher at a secular, liberal university, she met challenges to both her character and career daily. A genuine appreciation for the opportunities she was given strengthened her spirit in the toughest of these challenges. Further, her approach to change was profoundly different from the backbiting and mudslinging we see today. She reminded us to be cautious in our criticism. She understood the difficulty in putting forth new ideas and starting new organizations, and the minimal effort required to condemn. Lily called us to something higher: "If you want to change the world, change yourself." It is now time for us to think with gratitude for the bold witness Lily gave to us by her life of service to the Truth.

Marie Cabaud Meaney

INTERNATIONAL THEOLOGICAL INSTITUTE

Lily's friendship with my family crosses two generations. My father met her and her sister Louloute during his philosophy studies under Dietrich von Hildebrand at Fordham University. Their Francophone background, deep faith, and philosophical interests sealed their friendship as did their French wit and spirit of contradiction. Lily would get married to Dietrich von Hildebrand, and both were present at my parents' wedding. Famously, Dietrich—who was my father's best man—got side-tracked during his speech in honor of the married couple to make a fiery *laudatio* on Lily, whose birthday it was that day—something she reminded me almost every time I saw her.

After our move back to Europe, we would see Lily in southern Germany every summer for a gathering of like-minded people. She would hide her own insights and philosophical talents behind those of her then-deceased husband, claiming that everything came from him. In conversation with my mother in the late 1980s or early 1990s, I remember her once saying that she was missing her husband more over the years. Time had not mellowed, but intensified her pain.

I had the good luck to take a course on Kierkegaard in Gaming, Austria, with Lily in the early 1990s. On our one-day outing to Vienna, she peremptorily changed the program, saying that more time should be spent on the museum of art, the Kunsthistorisches Museum.

Furthermore, there was no sense in racing through the museum, which would inevitably lead to our forgetting everything we saw, she proclaimed. Instead, she would show us five paintings, which we should look at for twenty minutes, so that they would imprint themselves on our souls. I've been there so often since then that I'm not quite sure which ones they were, but I think Giorgione's *Adoration of the Shepherds*, Tintoretto's *Susanna and the Elders*, Bruegel's *Hunters in the Snow*, Veronese's *Jesus and the Samaritan Woman*, and Vermeer's *Artist*. I'm sure this visit left a lasting mark on all.

James Monti

AUTHOR AND HISTORIAN

Reflecting upon the prospect of her approaching death, Dr. von Hildebrand said she was in the final steps of her life, but that these steps were the most important. She asked me to pray not that she be granted a "good death," but rather a "holy death." She spoke of what she wanted her final words on Earth to be: "Thank you, I love you, and Forgive me."

Beth A. Rath

BORROMEO SEMINARY

In my last year at Franciscan University, I was finishing up my studies for a degree in philosophy and theology. Perhaps for the first time in my life, I was without a clear plan for my next steps. I loved learning, and I loved Christ and wanted to serve Him. I had a stack of nearly completed applications for Ph.D. programs in theology on my dorm room desk, but I lacked conviction that the Spirit was leading me for further study in theology.

Then I went to a lecture by Alice von Hildebrand. I can't remember the topic of the lecture itself, but one sentence from Professor von Hildebrand that day forever changed my life. As I recall it, she said, "If you want to open up the doors to God for people, you first have to combat moral relativism."

The words of Professor von Hildebrand cut to my heart in a way that facilitated an immediate "conversion." I threw away the graduate theology applications and began looking into Ph.D. programs in philosophy. I am deeply grateful to her for highlighting an important truth that day: philosophical errors are stumbling blocks to faith. That truth continues to inspire my work now as a seminary philosophy professor.

Fr. Francis Mary Roaldi

C.F.R., STUDENT OF ALICE VON HILDEBRAND

Among the many things that I gleaned from my friendship with Lily was the profound example of her last years on this earth. Back in 2004, Fr. Benedict Groeschel, C.F.R. called his good friend Lily to ask if she could tutor me. In the ensuing years, while I am quite certain that I rank very low among those who had the privilege of learning from her, I received much. But more recently, as she began to diminish in her intellectual strength, and her phenomenal memory became less clear, she taught me some of the greatest lessons. As I visited her almost monthly, over time she taught me how to leave this world as a person of faith.

Perhaps the most poignant memory is the following: we were chatting about a variety of topics, and we turned to one which always would light a fire for her: femininity. As we talked about it, I mentioned that someone had just told me they had read her work *The Privilege of Being a Woman* and loved it a great deal. I asked her about the central point of the book. She paused a while and then, with a big smile, said to me, "I can't remember." I was deeply moved. Not so much with sorrow but, rather, awe at the resignation and joy that she expressed in her poverty. Being a Franciscan, we are known for our joy and poverty. But that day, sitting in her apartment, Lily educated me a great deal about both of those. For this and the many other things God taught me through her I remain deeply grateful to Him.

Rev. Paul Scalia

CATHOLIC DIOCESE OF ARLINGTON

Lily met up to her billing. By the time I met her, early on in my priesthood, I already knew her writings and was a fan. What I found in her was not only that keen mind that loved to discuss the permanent things but also—and more importantly—a woman who was interested in you as a person. She could engage monumental issues of philosophy, theology, and art. But she was more concerned for you, your family, your work or vocation, and so on. It was never a conversation just about things but with people. At our first meeting she immediately asked about my family: How many siblings did I have? How many nieces and nephews? Any other vocations in the family? Ever keen on the dignity of woman and of motherhood, when I informed her about my somewhat large family (on the smaller side compared to many others she knew!), she responded, "I say congratulations—*to your mother!*"

Stephen D. Schwarz

UNIVERSITY OF RHODE ISLAND

Lily was a student of my father at Manhattanville College of the Sacred Heart, at that time in Uptown Manhattan. I was a little boy of ten. She immediately took me under her wing in a deep and affectionate love. She prayed with me and spoke of Christ's love for me. Later when I was older she spoke to me about philosophy. I was already connected to Dietrich von Hildebrand since he was my godfather and had been my father's teacher. But she brought me to a deeper awareness and appreciation of his philosophy. She has been a life-long friend and a companion on the philosophical journey opened up for us by von Hildebrand. I thank God for the great gift of this deep and long friendship.

Josef Seifert

DIETRICH VON HILDEBRAND INSTITUTE
OF REALIST PHENOMENOLOGY

I had the good fortune to have known Lily for seventy-four years (I met her at the age of just three). In 1948, Dietrich von Hildebrand (Gogo), who had fled to New York City as a refugee and public enemy of the Nazis, began to return annually to Europe during his summer vacations, financing his trip by being a most personable, extremely knowledgeable, and wonderful tour guide of his beloved Italy and Austria for interested students, among them Lily.

As my parents were friends of his, Gogo always spent some time in my parents' home, accompanied by some close friends, including Lily, whom he married in 1959. From their wedding on, Gogo and Lily spent part of their summer vacation each year together with my family in magnificent Italian settings such as Lake Garda (in Limone sul Garda), Bocca di Magra, near La Spezia and the Ligurian coast, and wonderful places like Cinque Terre.

At that time (at twelve through fourteen), I had become intensely interested in and fallen in love with Gogo's philosophy, a love Lily and I shared completely. These joint vacations and some get-togethers in Florence gave me a unique opportunity to get to know Gogo and his philosophy and Lily most closely. She was a wonderful wife to Gogo. They loved each other deeply and shared in a unique way all the truth, beauty, and philosophy, and intense *joie de vivre* and joy in their faith and daily Mass and communion, which both attended with the greatest fervor, though Lily more quietly and discreetly than Gogo, whose heart overflowed with his love of Christ and the Church and who expressed this love often in words.

Lily's books *Greek Culture* and *Introduction to a Philosophy of Religion* were very much a fruit of their dialogues and intensely shared reflections, which also continued in the villa San Francesco di Paola in Florence, Gogo's birthplace, where I had a unique opportunity to spend much time and to meet with and get to know Lily's profound philosophical talent, deep understanding of her husband's philosophy, her sense of humor and brilliant wittiness, and her sublime faith and love of Christ and the Catholic Church.

I also encountered Lily's brilliant mind and great gift as a teacher when I sat in on some of her classes at Hunter College in New York City during the spring semester of 1966, which I spent in the home of Lily's sister Louloute and her family in New Rochelle, just five minutes on foot from Lily and Gogo's apartment.

My most wonderful recollections of Lily, however, those that make her most present to me, date from her last few years when I could visit her every year briefly in New Rochelle. During these visits, which she always received gladly, though they began to become a burden as her health weakened in the mid and late 1990s, she was filled with a patience I had never before noted in her to that extent, especially in the midst of her increasing sufferings, and with a deep gratitude for everything, including my visits. She still took a vivid part in all the philosophical activities and human events of my life, with an extraordinary cordiality and gratitude for all the gifts she had received in her life. During these years she seemed even kinder and more patient, more filled with that deep charity, on which her husband had written so wonderfully.

These last memories are the sweetest I have, even after her memory and mind, which had been so incredibly sharp up into her mid-nineties, began to fail. I recall how after a long visit, she recommended that I get to know a very good and well-known young Austrian philosopher. When I asked her for his name, she said my name and laughed very sweetly when I told her that this man was myself (though far from young by then!).

I am deeply convinced that she now lives in the eternal presence of God, for whom she ardently longed, united in the fulfillment of all love with her husband, family, and friends. If she is not yet in heaven, she is at least, I am sure, very close to entering the door to heavenly bliss.

Vivian Warren

BRUDERHOF

Lily taught me to think about womanhood and femininity in a completely new way, and my conversations with her were pivotal in the development of my attitude as a woman. She had absolutely no use for the modern feminist movement's emphasis on self-sufficiency and independence from men, remarking that the drive for "equality" with men was a telling sign of the lie of feminism: if women were truly confident in their femininity, they would not strive to be like men but would embrace the unique gifts of womanhood. To Lily being a woman was the most wonderful and awe-inspiring thing in the world. She loved to talk about how man was made from "the slime of the earth" (albeit then imbued with the breath of God) but woman was made from man (Genesis 2:7). She spoke of Adam being awed at the sight of Eve, and calling her "the mother of the living" (Genesis 3:20).

But while Lily was given a unique gift in being able to bring great thoughts to expression, she was at the same time one of the most humble, unassuming people I have ever met. She struggled with the same fear of death and of standing before the throne of God that all mortals do. In recent years she always spoke of her last steps and would say, "Pray for old ladies. The last steps are the hardest." It was her ardent prayer that she would be taken when she was at her most thankful, with the words "thank you" on her lips.

I wasn't there when she finally crossed over on January 14, 2022, but I am sure those were the words on her lips, because when you live your whole life with the kind of grace and humility and thankfulness she did, you will also enter the next world in peace and joy.

Thank you, Lily. You have taught me more than you will ever know.

Maria Seifert Wolter

FRANCISCAN UNIVERSITY OF STEUBENVILLE

I must have been seven or eight years old. Lily, my god-mother, presented me with a gift for my birthday. Her face was all joyous expectation as she watched me unwrap it. I did, and a beautiful hardcover copy of *The Hobbit* emerged. I was admiring it when all of a sudden she declared: "I am *so jealous!!*" (in her French-Belgian accent). I was quite perplexed and thought perhaps I ought to offer to give the book back. But before I could say anything she continued: "*You* get to read it for the first time!" She said it with so much enthusiasm and awe that that statement has always stayed with me. It is on account of her remark that I have so often stopped and paused to enter into the *first* time more consciously and intentionally. She captured some-thing so very intriguing and important. There is some-thing special and uniquely unrepeatable about experienc-ing something the *first* time.

HOMILY FOR THE FUNERAL MASS OF ALICE VON HILDEBRAND

By Fr. Gerald E. Murray
Church of the Holy Family, New Rochelle, New York
January 22, 2022

"Therefore, since we are justified by faith, we have peace
with God through our Lord Jesus Christ. Through him
we have obtained access to this grace in which we stand,
and we rejoice in our hope of sharing the glory of God."

—*Letter of St. Paul the Apostle to the Romans* (5:1–2)

As we join together in prayer at this Requiem Mass for the
repose of the soul of our beloved friend and mentor Alice
von Hildebrand, known as "Lily" to her friends, we pray
that she who had such deep faith in the truth who is our
Lord Jesus Christ, that she who radiated the peace that

God bestows on those who love Him, may now see the fulfillment of her hope, sharing in the glory that God bestows on His good and faithful servants who have received the supreme gift of the beatific vision, seeing God face to face.

Before the body of a deceased Catholic is brought to the parish church for the Requiem Mass, the Church offers this prayer at the wake: "O Lord, we commend to you the soul of your servant Alice, that having departed from this world, she may live with you. And by the grace of your merciful love, wash away the sins that in human frailty she has committed in the conduct of her life." Lily asked for Masses to be offered for her soul. She was very conscious of the need that sinners have to seek God's pardon. In December of 2016 she told a friend: "You know, I have lived a long life. I will tell you a secret. I am ready for it to be over. I think I have done what God wanted me to do. If I died tomorrow, I think I would be grateful. Also, I am a coward: I am afraid of what is coming. I pray for the younger generation. I think we are coming back around in history when people will be killed for their faith. If you are there when I am on my deathbed remind me to say, forgive me my sins, thank you to God, and I love you. Have you ever thought about the words you will say on your deathbed? Of course, not; you are too young but for me it is very close." She was off by only five years in predicting her departure from this vale of tears. Those five years, indeed all her ninety-eight years on earth, were a gift from God both to Lily and to all those who loved her. Her gratitude to God for all He did for her in this life never wavered but, rather, grew stronger. She marveled at her long life as she marveled at everything that God did for her.

In August of 2017 Lily told a friend: "I love the story of Abraham, how Isaac asked him on the way to the mount where God had told him to sacrifice his son, 'but where is the sacrifice?' and Abraham responded, 'God will provide.' That is how I feel about my death—God will provide the right people and the right circumstances." The Lord did indeed provide for her as Holy Mass was celebrated in her apartment, and she received the Anointing of the Sick and the Apostolic Pardon, on January 13th. She went to the Lord that very night, shortly after midnight.

Her death brings to an earthly close a truly amazing life. Born in 1923, her journey through this world into the world to come took her in 1940 from her native Belgium to New York, in flight from the Nazi invaders. Her first home here was at the Waldorf Astoria Hotel with her aunt and uncle. Little did she know then that she would spend thirty-eight years at a nearby secular school, Hunter College, teaching philosophy. It was her love of books and learning that led her to Manhattanville College of the Sacred Heart and then to Fordham University, where she studied philosophy under the guidance of the brilliant and courageous Dietrich von Hildebrand, who had fled Munich for Vienna when Adolf Hitler and his Nazi party took power in Germany. His writings against the Nazis put him at the top of the Gestapo list of people to be arrested when the German army marched into Austria. He escaped on the last train out of Vienna and made his way to New York, where he resumed his work as a philosopher and as a

Catholic writer and speaker who inspired his students and friends with a deep love of Christ, of the Church, and, in particular, of the Church's sacred liturgy.

Lily soon became his secretary, and after von Hildebrand's wife Margarete died in 1957, he asked her to marry him in 1959. They eventually moved to New Rochelle and were members of this parish of the Holy Family. My family were also parishioners here. I remember as a grammar schoolboy wondering who this couple was as they sat a few pews ahead of our family at Sunday Mass. I was to find out, to my great benefit, a few years later, when I decided to enter the seminary to study for the priesthood. I discovered the greatness of these two philosophers who defended all that is worth defending so that man may live at peace with himself, with others, and with God.

One of the most central themes in the lives of Dietrich and Alice von Hildebrand was the crucial importance of reverence if man is to order his life properly and fruitfully in this world. Lily wrote extensively about matters of faith in various Catholic publications in the years that followed her retirement in 1984 from teaching at Hunter College. Reverence was a central topic. Let me cite three passages from her articles.

1. "The curse of modern men is that so many of them have lost their sense for wonder and gratitude. Boredom is a punishment for irreverence. Alas, our mind-boggling technological progress has brought with it the curse of taking things for granted and assuming with blind stupidity that there is nothing we cannot know—nothing that

he cannot master. Having a small gadget in his hand, one feels that he is the master of the universe. He can click on a button and have the world at his fingertips. Regretfully, we never hear homilists say a word about the sin of being 'blasé.' It is a sin because it is a consequence of ingratitude—because it is a fruit of pride and metaphysical arrogance. Every sin brings with it its own punishment." ("Reverence: The Mother of All Virtue," Catholic News Agency, April 26, 2016.)

2. "What is 'reverence?' It is an uplifting and joyful feeling of awe, a response that man is called upon to give to God's creation which clearly points to the Creator; it is an ever renewed and grateful discovery of the mysteries of being; it is an overcoming of one's moral blindness preventing us from perceiving the glories of the universe that we live in. It is a joy to perceive how marvelous it is 'to be,' and consequently, should make us respond with horror at abortion, willingly and brutally denying existence to others (for I doubt that abortionists would have chosen to be aborted themselves had they had a chance of doing it.) They deny life to others, not to themselves. We all should tremble with respect at perceiving a little creature making its dramatic entrance into our world." (Ibid.)

3. "Irreverence is spreading through modern society like a cancer. It is metastasizing and has infected virtually every facet of our everyday life. The authentic meaning of 'culture' refers to a refinement, an elevation, a spiritualization of everyday life—that is, it aims to put the seal of the Spirit on our daily activities. Today, however, the word 'culture' refers to whatever has been most recently

produced. We have forgotten that true culture elevates; it does not drag down. I dare say that much of what we see today is an *anti-culture*. It certainly cannot be read as a *sursum corda* (Lift up your hearts)—a call to look upward, triggering gratitude in our souls. It was typical of Plato's genius that he would warn us that one of the main aims of education is to train a child to 'love what is lovable, and hate what is mean and ugly.' This is the antidote to the disease of irreverence that is ravaging our society and sickening our culture. When will we avail ourselves of it?" ("The Disease of Irreverence," *New Oxford Review*, June 2011.)

Lily's love for the truth was a fruit of her love for Christ, who is the Truth. She did not speak about Catholicism in the classroom at Hunter, a secular school. She taught philosophy not theology. But her students who heard about the existence of objective truth in her classes were free to ask themselves questions about the origin of truth. And that led a good number of them to seek answers beyond philosophy. Lily recounted one incident that occurred shortly before she retired:

"Not long ago, in my 'Introduction to Philosophy' course, I was discussing truth. I gave my students the classical argument against subjectivism and relativism, namely, that whenever one tries to deny objective truth one must simultaneously claim that one's own statement is itself true, really and objectively. Suddenly, a male student raised his hand, rose (a most unusual occurrence), and said in a strong, clear voice: 'I object, Professor, to your spreading Roman Catholicism in this classroom.' There followed a

moment of great tension and my thoughts rushed to God
for help. Then I said quietly: 'I'm afraid that you are guilty
of an anachronism.' Since the student in question did not
know what it meant, I explained: 'The argument I have
been using is taken from Plato, who lived some four centuries before the birth of Christ. He can hardly be called
a Roman Catholic. This should answer your objection.' I
then proceeded with my teaching. Some sixteen months
later I received a phone call just as I was about to leave for
the university, where I was scheduled to proctor exams
for the evening. The person who was calling, a former student, said she urgently wanted to see me. I told her that
this was not possible since I was to be on duty the whole
evening and, furthermore, it was my last day at the university until the fall term. She started to cry over the phone
and insisted that she had to see me immediately. Surmising
that her problem was truly serious, I contacted a friend of
mine who agreed to proctor in my stead.

"I then rushed to the university. I hardly had time to
take off my coat when the girl who had phoned me came
in. I immediately recognized her even though she had never spoken to me personally when she was my student. She
had a fine, sensitive face, and I had been impressed by her
attentiveness and eagerness to listen. To my utter amazement, she told me abruptly that she wanted to become a
Roman Catholic. I was so surprised that I was speechless,
but I then decided to test her. 'Why?' I asked. 'Your courses
convinced me.' 'But,' I responded, 'I didn't say a word about
religion in my classes; my topic is philosophy.' 'I know,' she
answered, 'but do you recall an incident about sixteen

months ago when a student got up and objected to your refutation of subjectivism and relativism on the ground that you were spreading Roman Catholicism in the classroom? I had been brought up with strong anti-Catholic prejudices. But just when the student spoke out, the grace of God struck me. I suddenly understood that the Roman Catholic Church *does* stand for the objectivity of truth and that I had been blinded by prejudices.

'Your course helped me very much and I decided to take another one with you,' she continued. 'I heard through another student that you were the wife of a famous Roman Catholic writer, Dietrich von Hildebrand. I rushed to the library and read a couple of his works. Now I am convinced. Please, help me to find a good priest so that I can take instructions in the faith.'

"This is how L. C. found her way into the Church. I learned a great lesson through her experience: God is so powerful, so great, that He can use anything for the good." ("Classroom Conversion," *National Catholic Register*, March 20, 1983.)

We give thanks to God for the life of our dear departed friend Lily von Hildebrand. We owe her many debts of gratitude for all that she did for us and for countless others who learned, and will continue to learn, from her example, her writings, and her public speeches and media appearances, especially on EWTN. She taught us how to live, and how to die. May she rest in God's peace, knowing the One who made her, redeemed her, and has now called her to Himself.

ALICE VON HILDEBRAND,
WOMAN OF VALOR

⟶

By Rabbi Mark Gottlieb

First Things, March 1, 2022

Those who knew Alice von Hildebrand ("Lily" to her family and friends) could be forgiven for thinking she might outlive—possibly by a wide mark—the ninety-nine years given to her by her beloved maker. When she passed away in January in her apartment in New Rochelle, New York, mourners were grateful for having known such a remarkable woman and almost incredulous that this preternaturally energetic presence was now gone.

Born Alice Jourdain to a devoutly Catholic family in Belgium in 1923, Lily and her older sister, Louloute, would escape Europe in 1940 on the last passenger vessel to leave France. She had something of a religious experience when the boat was almost sunk by a German submarine; her brush with death convinced her of God's goodness, taking her to a place where "time vanishes and everything is present." Upon arriving in the United States, Lily lived with her aunt and uncle at the Waldorf Astoria but found little in life to give her joy or meaning. This changed one evening when she was introduced to the German-Italian convert and philosopher Dietrich von Hildebrand and his circle of friends. "After twenty-nine months of darkness," Lily would write in *Memoirs of a Happy Failure*, "the sun again rose in my life." Lily and Dietrich eventually married in 1959, and worked together to advance Catholic spiritual and intellectual life until Dietrich's passing in 1977.

Lily's own passion for ideas propelled her to a decades-long vocation as a professor of philosophy at Hunter College. She was popular in the classroom but often resented in the faculty room for raising questions about the regnant philosophical fads of the day. "There is one absolute dogma in the liberal world, namely the universal relativity and subjectivity of all values," she wrote. "To challenge this dogma is already to violate the separation of church and state."

After Lily retired, she began to develop her understanding of femininity and what she would call the "terrible lie of Feminism" in her books, *The Privilege of Being a Woman* and *Man and Woman: A Divine Invention*. Always analytically sophisticated and attentive to lived reality, Lily warned her readers that despite the fatal flaws in contemporary feminism, her own account of femininity should not be misrepresented in an absolutist fashion, since "generalizations are usually indicative of a mediocre mind" and "sweeping statements about 'all men' or 'all women' are redolent of prejudice and superficiality."

One of Lily's favorite biblical texts was the Song of the Valiant Woman, Solomon's paean to womanhood in Proverbs 31: "What a rare find is a virtuous woman, more precious than rubies." St. Hilary, bishop of Poitiers and an early doctor of the Church, follows Origen in reading the narrative allegorically. For Hilary, the woman is Wisdom, *Sapientia*, aiding man in his journey toward virtue. In Lily, womanhood and wisdom were one, the artifact of humility and grace.

The Torah, in its plain meaning, also insists that the woman of valor values the friendship of other women. In Lily's case, this could not be more evident than in the nearly eighty-year friendship she enjoyed with Madeleine Froelicher Stebbins, herself a great champion of tradition and beauty. Lily and Madeleine met at one of von Hildebrand's evening lectures in his apartment when the two were still in their early twenties. According to Lily, "[s]he was so radiant, pure, enchanting, feminine, graceful, and warmhearted that I immediately thought, 'I wish she were my friend.'"

In life and in death, these souls were deeply connected. Lily is now buried next to her husband but also beside Madeleine (who passed away late last year). When I first saw the twin gravestones, they recalled for me a day about a decade ago when the two women invited me for lunch at Madeleine's apartment in Westchester. They went out of their way for me and bought kosher food at the Jewish market in a neighboring town (only later did I learn that Madeleine's parents were involved in a Catholic network that helped save 3,000 Jews from Germany and Austria in the late 1930s). It was a delightful few hours, and our conversation ranged from updates about my growing family to the Orthodox Jewish theologian Michael Wyschogrod's intellectual debt to Heidegger, something that troubled Lily greatly. As much as she respected her colleague from Hunter College—one of the few colleagues she did respect—she couldn't understand why a God-fearing intellectual, let alone an Orthodox Jew, was attracted to the thought of a Nazi-colluding magus (the great Rabbi Joseph Soloveitchik expressed similar antipathy but studied Heidegger's philosophy more carefully, I suspect).

Lily could be stubborn at times, with a touch of triumphalism, displaying the holy indignation you'd expect from a fierce culture warrior and defender of the Church Militant; Madeleine was the more genteel and softer of the pair. The sight of these two ladies together—spiritual sisters as much as worldly friends, Catholic royalty and laity both—left a deep impression on me. As Lily once said, "Love and friendship are the remnants of the earthly Paradise." It certainly felt that way in their company.

However allegorically we may want to read Proverbs 31, an ancient Jewish hermeneutical principle insists that scripture cannot be shorn of its contextual sense or meaning. Which brings us back to Lily as life partner and peer of her beloved husband, Dietrich von Hildebrand. In addition to being a remarkable teacher, thinker, and culture warrior in her own right, Lily was a faithful steward of her husband's philosophical legacy after his death (though she once suggested that her late husband's Germanic mien prevented him from appreciating her sometimes mischievous French wit).

My own friendship with Lily emerged, unsurprisingly, from my early interest in her husband's work and witness. I first encountered von Hildebrand's thought thirty-five years ago—though not through his heroic anti-Nazi writings, which may have been inspiring to a young philo-Catholic Jew like myself. Instead, one of my dear rabbis gave me a copy of *The New Tower of Babel*, a trenchant critique of modernity, and told me to read the essay "Beauty in the Light of the Redemption." My rebbe knew I was grappling with vexing questions on the theological value of beauty and that von Hildebrand was a vital source. But when I finally met Lily years later, our friendship was as transformative as anything I had read in her late husband's consequential body of writing. Lily's life was one of consummate grace, fierce intelligence, and beauty—a life I could learn from in direct relationship, more than through book knowledge.

In 2013, Lily celebrated her ninetieth birthday by delivering a talk, "Gratitude as the Key to Happiness." In it, she said that on the topic of gratitude, she was merely a faithful recorder of her husband's teachings. Gratitude, according to von Hildebrand, was the natural response of the soul to the goodness inherent in another person, especially the ultimate Person. "Like hope," von Hildebrand avers, "the affective response of gratitude implies a tacit reliance on the existence of a benevolent and all-powerful

God, even by those who have not yet found Him." In characteristically accessible yet profound language, Lily added: "Any day that is without 'thank you' is lost." Let us not lose the opportunity to thank our maker for giving us the gift of Alice von Hildebrand, who arduously defended the truth through her formidable faculties of head and heart.

ALICE VON HILDEBRAND: LITTLE BUT FIERCE

By Rachel Bulman

Word on Fire, January 28, 2022

"We are dwarfs sitting on the shoulders of giants."
—John of Salsberg

When I read the words of Alice von Hildebrand, I often imagine a tall, looming figure with an overpowering personality whose keen wit and sharp tongue could defeat even the most foreboding enemy. Her words are laden with conviction and knowledge, set forth before the audiences of women (and men) searching—aching to connect to the fullness of who they are in a world that is loud yet unclear amid society's woes and limited, utilitarian focus.

I stumbled upon her on YouTube. There she was, speaking in 2010, sitting behind a broad table meant for five, a seemingly frail and aged woman, small in stature. She opened her mouth to speak, and wisdom filled the room. Her heart poured into that conference and made clear the words often quoted from Shakespeare's *Midsummer Night's Dream*: "Though she be but little she is fierce."

Alice was a philosopher, feminist, author, lecturer, and teacher, but before all of this (in fact, what shaped most of her work) came her life as the wife of Dietrich von Hildebrand, the personalist philosopher that even Hitler feared.

"All the work that I've done ... [is] based on what my husband taught me," she said. Alice met Dietrich in 1942, and she became his secretary and his student. They married in 1959, two years after the death of his first wife of forty-five years. Their love for each other, for the Catholic Church, and for objective truth would enrich their lives and the lives of so many others. She spent her last years translating her husband's work into English and entrusting this lifelong promotion to the Hildebrand Project in 2015.

When she wasn't promoting her husband's work, Alice spent most of her life reminding women of the privilege of femininity and the gift of motherhood. Her most popular work is arguably *The Privilege of Being a Woman*.

Secularism, materialism, and utilitarianism have so infected our society that men and women fall victim to their sway daily. Alice would say that men were the first victims, falsely accepting the commonplace notion that success is defined by worldly values like money, power, and fame. Then as men commuted from their homes and immediate neighborhoods to pursue "success," the -isms of the world invaded the hearts of the women as well. We were told that if we didn't want to be left behind—if we too wanted to be relevant under this definition of success—we needed to pursue it by way of these established values, leaving many women to believe they must become like men in order to be successful, to have value, and to be seen. Inevitably those occupations considered "feminine," particularly if they were centered on the home, began to be seen as weak, less meaningful, and of dubious value in the eyes of the world.

The feminism taught by Alice offered a new path under the guidance of our Blessed Virgin Mary, who offered two very striking phrases that shape much of what femininity should model: "Be it done unto me according to thy word" and "Do whatever he tells you." This new path is built upon the feminine genius of receptivity and invitation. The first phrase reminds us of the full receptivity of Mary and that the fullness of grace shaped her mission. The latter phrase is set in the context of the Wedding at Cana. Mary alerted Jesus to the lack of wine, and then she turned to the servants with this phrase. This standalone phrase could be mistaken for an argument for wanton submission, but instead it is said by Our Lady, in full awareness of the need of the moment, understanding the way to fulfill the lack, and using this wisdom to invite others into that battlefield—her Son and the servants.

Alice invited women to *be* women, to have their power rooted in their own femininity. She believed that women could be receptive, nurturing, demure, and empathetic while also wielding the dynamism of intellect and culture.

She contributed greatly to philosophy and paved the

path for other women to become teachers and lovers of wisdom themselves. In a recent interview with the *National Catholic Register*, a former student of Alice's called her "one of those outstanding female figures of Catholic life in the US in the 20th century." And though she had no children of her own, Alice was the spiritual mother to many young women, including myself.

Though I never had the honor of meeting her—and I do have children, and the busy life that goes with them— the words that she has written and many of her talks have shaped my own understanding of who I am and what I am capable of, much more than I would have imagined without her help. Two particular works have been especially helpful to me: *The Privilege of Being a Woman* and *By Love Refined: Letters to a Young Bride*.

In *The Privilege*, Alice gives us nine essays exploring everything from the denigration of women, to the female body, to an exploration of our feelings. It's a quick read and pertinent to the Christian understanding of femininity—particularly the opening chapters, which present arguments for and against the privilege of being a woman.

By Love Refined is a collection of letters written to a young bride. Lily (as Alice was known to her close friends) penned more than sixty letters to "Julie" during her first year of marriage. I'd suggest every married woman read this brilliant collection of letters. You can take in one a day and double (or triple!) up on the days when you have extra time. Alice tackles everything from what to do when you like things that your husband hates to how to handle the disappointment of the anniversary dinner being canceled because of unforeseen circumstances.

Beyond these two renowned works, Alice was and will continue to be a much needed female voice in the field of philosophy, bringing to the light the need for a new language of feminism long before Pope St. John Paul II enriched the terminology in his 1988 apostolic letter *Mulieris dignitatem*. She taught me that women do not need to all but become men in order to be empowered, but that femininity contains and wields a necessary power in and of itself. She also continues to inspire me toward a male/female complementarity that simultaneously honors the male and female differentiation while upholding gender equality. This was a thread not only woven into all of her lectures and talks but also lived out in her marriage to Dietrich.

If you search for Alice's work on Amazon today, her books have all skyrocketed in price, showing that many are finding her feminine voice echoing into the world even louder in the wake of her death. That voice not only asks us to discover the philosophy of personalism and a rightly ordered new feminism, but it also lightly whispers introductions to some of the greatest thinkers of our time, including Thomas à Kempis, Gertrud von Le Fort, Gabriel Marcel, and, most of all, Dietrich von Hildebrand.

It is amazing to note that this tiny, frail woman seemed to fill every seat on the five-person table during the talk I mentioned at the start of this article. Her wisdom and strength were not found in her own merit of mind or body but in embracing that aging frailty, the littleness, the so-called weakness, and allowing it to be transformed by grace. Like our Lady, Alice (though never bearing children of her own) allowed the figurative womb of her intellect to be filled with the Person of Christ, and bore him to the world. His face and heart radiated in all of her work. I find joy in knowing that through that womb, I became a child of Alice von Hildebrand.

CATHOLIC PHILOSOPHER ALICE VON HILDEBRAND DIDN'T NEED TO PROSELYTIZE TO BRING HER STUDENTS TO GOD

By John F. Crosby

America Magazine, March 10, 2022

Dietrich von Hildebrand is well known as an eminent Catholic phenomenologist; he had the same teachers as St. Edith Stein, and his work in phenomenological philosophy is no less important than hers. He is also known for his groundbreaking work on marriage and for his religious writings, including his classic work *Transformation in Christ*. In addition, he has always been recognized as one of the strongest Catholic voices against Hitler in 1930s Europe.

But the story of this great man is not complete without

the story of his remarkable wife, Alice Jourdain von Hildebrand, who died in January 2022 at the age of ninety-eight.

She did not only stand devotedly next to her famous husband; she was a real collaborator with him. She understood his thought from within. After his death in 1977, Alice devoted the rest of her life to making his philosophical and theological legacy known. She found imaginative ways of bringing his thought to audiences that he did not reach, as in the many programs she did for EWTN over the years. But she was more than a collaborator, and more than a custodian of his legacy; she spoke with a voice of her own. She and her husband formed a presence in the Catholic world not unlike that of Jacques and Raïssa Maritain.

Alice Jourdain von Hildebrand was born in Belgium in 1923. In 1940, she fled with her family to France ahead of the advancing German army. In the summer of 1940, her parents, fearing for the safety of their daughters, put her and her sister on a ship bound for New York. The ship was stopped by a German submarine not far from Ireland. Everyone was ordered into lifeboats and the Germans threatened to sink the ship; Alice was certain that she and her sister were about to die. But when the Germans saw that the passengers were all refugees, they allowed it to pass.

In 1942, she heard a talk in New York by Dietrich von Hildebrand on transformation in Christ. It was an encounter that opened to her a new world and a new life. Though she had been raised in a devout Catholic home, she had never heard anyone speak about life in Christ with such ardor. Many people had this encounter with von Hildebrand.

I myself had it in 1966. Along with the renewal of her faith, Alice discovered her gift for philosophy. She studied with von Hildebrand at Fordham, completing her doctorate with a dissertation on St. Augustine in 1949. She wanted to teach philosophy and applied, unsuccessfully, to various Catholic colleges in the New York area. To her surprise, she found a temporary position at Hunter College in New York City.

Alice was at first reluctant to teach in a totally secular academic environment. She had always lived among Catholics and had been raised in Belgium in a refined and sheltered milieu. She had never dealt with people like the students at Hunter College in the 1940s, some of whom were rough around the edges and not exactly well mannered. But soon she found herself drawn precisely to these students. Alice looked past all the cultural barriers that separated her from them, and she entered into their griefs and hopes. She understood her students' spiritual hunger. She had a heart for them in all their brokenness. And they were drawn to her. Many of them turned to her with their personal needs. Many found their way to God through her teaching. And so it happened that her temporary position of a few weeks turned into a 37-year teaching career at Hunter.

She resolved never to bring her Catholic faith explicitly into the classroom. She hewed closely to the methods of philosophy. How, then, does one explain the conversions among her students? Alice put it like this: she would present the arguments of Plato and Aristotle against relativism. Her students grasped the force of these arguments. She found that for many of them it was a short and easy step from the objective validity of truth to God. It was the relativism that was keeping them from God; as soon as that obstacle was removed, faith became a live option for them. Friedrich Nietzsche would have understood well what she was doing, for he realized that whoever venerates objective truth is already a theist. This is why his atheism required him to replace the will to truth with the will to power, and this is why Alice von Hildebrand was able to undermine atheism by reviving the will to truth.

But there is something else that explains the extraordinary resonance that she found with her students at Hunter: her rare pedagogical talents. She was gifted with a sharp Gallic wit (something that her husband did not have). This gave her a certain charm in the classroom and made her formidable in discussion and debate, even though in appearance she was slight and frail. Once, a student was trying to provoke her by saying that human beings are directly descended from the apes and differ only in degree from them. After trying in vain to respond with philosophical arguments, she resorted to her wit: "Well, if it turns out to be true, I'd accept it, but I wouldn't brag about it."

On another occasion, someone complained that a certain article she had written was rather weak, to which she retorted, "Well, you know, only mediocre people are always at their best." She never used her wit to humiliate, but always to engender warmth. She combined in herself wit, wisdom, and warmth in such a way as to be able to engage her students at a deep level. Even during the student unrest at Hunter in 1970, when Hunter College was officially closed, she continued to hold her classes, and her students continued to turn up for them.

But her colleagues were another story. She recounted in her 2014 autobiography, *Memoirs of a Happy Failure*, that many of them resented her, and many of the department chairs and deans whom Alice served seemed to want to make life so miserable for her that she would leave. It may have been because of envy—none of her colleagues had anything like the student following that she had.

But most of all, it was because of her Catholicism, she wrote; the other professors said that she was proselytizing, indoctrinating her students so as to win them over for the Church. Her memoir recounts episodes in which colleagues told students to avoid her classes or sent student spies into her classes to collect evidence of proselytizing. Further, Alice wrote, her colleagues at Hunter maligned her, confined her to teaching evening sessions, and tried to block her tenure; she also thought it highly likely that letters favorable to her that disappeared from her personnel file were destroyed by her adversaries. (*America* reached out to Hunter College for comment on these allegations but received no response.)

But as I said, she was resolved not to mention the Church in her classes. She responded instead with the resources of philosophy to the crisis of meaning that so many of her students were suffering. Most of her critics knew nothing of the life-giving power of authentic philosophy. They taught philosophy without attending to the sapiential

dimension of it, and so they could find no other explana-
tion for the religious awakening among her students than
inappropriate proselytizing.

But the charge of proselytizing did not find much trac-
tion with the students. In 1984, Hunter decided to give an
award for outstanding teaching. Over 800 faculty members
were eligible, and the students voted: she won the award.

At the same time that Alice Jourdain was reaching
out to disoriented and despairing souls at Hunter College, another great Catholic woman was at work in New
York City. Dorothy Day was leading the Catholic Worker
movement with its outreach to the homeless, the destitute,
the hungry. She highly esteemed the writings of Dietrich
von Hildebrand, whom she often quoted in the pages of
The Catholic Worker, but as far as I know she did not know
about Alice and her work at Hunter. But were these two
Catholic women not fighting the same fight, just on different fronts? Were they not sisters in the spirit? Did not
each of them, in her own way, practice a ministry to the
neediest?

I have mainly spoken of Alice von Hildebrand as an inspired teacher of philosophy; but she was also an author.
Particularly noteworthy are her writings on man and
woman—writings such as *The Privilege of Being a Woman*
and *Man and Woman: A Divine Invention*. She attempted in
these books something like what St. Edith Stein attempted
in her well-known papers on womanhood.

Both were Catholic women philosophers trying to re-
think the identity and role of women in response to the
epochal stirring of thought about sex and gender in our

time. Alice von Hildebrand wrote with perhaps more of a polemical edge than Stein did, but what she wrote is full of wisdom. She spoke with a voice that deserves to be heard today.

We Catholics should keep track of the heroes of faith in our time and should cherish their memory. Let us remember not only Dietrich von Hildebrand, but also his wife, Alice.

ALICE VON HILDEBRAND:
A BRIEF BIOGRAPHY

Alice Marie (née Jourdain) von Hildebrand, known to family and friends as "Lily," was born in Brussels, Belgium, on March 11, 1923. The third of five children (three sisters and one brother), she was educated by the Canonesses of Saint Augustine in Brussels. Her native language was French. She died peacefully at home in New Rochelle, New York, on January 14, 2022.

When the Nazis invaded Belgium in May 1940, Lily (then seventeen) and her four siblings fled with their parents to Bordeaux. From there, at the invitation of her aunt and uncle living in New York City, she and her eldest sister Louloute were able to board the *SS Washington*, the last passenger vessel to depart France during the war. While sailing from Lisbon to Galway to pick up additional refugees, the *SS Washington* was intercepted by a German U-boat. On deck, faced with the prospect of death, Lily had a life-changing experience. Looking out onto the "mysterious, fog-covered Atlantic, ... with a clarity and precision that approached the supernatural, all of a sudden, in a single flash, I relived everything I had ever done, failed to do, thought, imagined, felt. The experience was overwhelming and convinced me of God's goodness. Could I not assume that, at the very moment of death, God would grant this experience to everyone, so that each person would have the chance to say, 'have mercy on me, my Lord'?" The captain of the *SS Washington* was eventually able to convince the U-boat commander that he was carrying refugees, and they were permitted to continue their journey, arriving in New York Harbor on June 21, 1940.

The six years she spent with her aunt and uncle, despite living with them in the Waldorf Astoria in New York, were extraordinarily difficult for Lily. She was thought unfit for further studies, and even sent to secretarial school. Eventually, she was allowed to enroll at Manhattanville College. One of her philosophy professors there was Balduin Schwarz, a student of Dietrich von Hildebrand, who invited Lily to attend a talk by Dietrich on November 27, 1942. Dietrich spoke on "the readiness to change," a theme in his great religious work *Transformation in Christ*. This encounter became the great turning point of Lily's life. "From the first moment he began to speak, I felt that he was feeding my soul with a food that I had always longed for. He spoke out of a deep recollection, and I drank in every word.... After twenty-nine months of darkness, the sun again rose in my life."

Even before completing her B.A., Lily began taking classes with Dietrich at Fordham University in 1943. She became acquainted with Dietrich's first wife, Margarete (who died in 1957), and became an integral member of the Hildebrands' circle of friends. Soon after beginning her studies with Dietrich, she began to assist him as his secretary. Over the coming decades, she typed many of his book manuscripts (which he always wrote by hand) and translated a number of his essays into English. She is surely the reason certain works saw the light of day. Not only did she supply most of the footnotes for his books; she became a true philosophical collaborator, reading and discussing his works in progress.

When her aunt and uncle returned to Belgium in 1946, she was forced to accompany them. Determined to complete her studies, she persuaded her parents to let her go back to New York. This time, she was living not in the splendor of the Waldorf Astoria but in a modest apartment with Madeleine Froelicher (later Stebbins), who would be her closest friend for nearly eighty years. They met in the fall of 1943 at one of Dietrich's evening lectures. Lily never forgot that first impression: "She was so radiant, pure, enchanting, feminine, graceful, and warmhearted that I immediately thought, 'I wish she were my friend.'"

As Lily's resources dwindled, she desperately searched for a teaching position at Catholic colleges around New York. Despite excellent credentials, she was repeatedly told: "It is not the policy of Catholic colleges to appoint women to teach philosophy." But she was introduced to the chairman of the philosophy department at Hunter College in New York, who hired her for a three-week substitute position in December of 1947. She prepared for those first classes with "the intensity that only despair can fuel." Despite being certain of having failed, after those three weeks she was offered a position in a new Hunter College veterans program in the Bronx.

Thus began a teaching career at Hunter College that would span thirty-seven years. From the start, she faced opposition from her own colleagues, in part out of professional rivalry (she quickly became one of the most popular professors) and in part because of anti-Catholic sentiment. The latter surprised her because she never spoke of Catholicism in the classroom. The difficulty was that several of her students began converting to Catholicism. She soon realized that it was her defense of the objectivity of truth against the prevailing relativism of the day that prepared the ground for these conversions. "If someone finds the truth, he automatically finds God, because God *is* the truth."

Lily retired from Hunter College in the spring of 1984. Just as the semester was winding down, she received a call from Hunter president Donna Shalala, informing her that she had received the highest student evaluation in the college (from among 850 teachers) and would receive the award for Excellence in Teaching during graduation at Madison Square Garden.

Lily had married Dietrich in July 1959. She often spoke of their unique partnership: complete unity in love of philosophy, music, literature, art, and, above all, their Catholic faith. They had a great love for the sacrality of the liturgy and the Church's heritage of sacred music. Together they formed an extraordinary team in bearing witness to Christian culture and Christian life.

In the years after her retirement from teaching, she lectured in thirty-five U.S. states, Canada, Mexico, and in many countries in South America and Europe. In these years she also began to develop her understanding of femininity—informed by her husband's thought on love but also distinctively her own, as expressed principally in her books *The Privilege of Being a Woman* and *Man and Woman: A Divine Invention*. Her book *By Grief Refined* was borne of the experience of becoming a widow with Dietrich's death in 1977. In addition to her book *Introduction to the Philosophy of Religion*, she has left behind a rich body of essays on the nature of education, reverence, liturgy, marriage, and many other themes. She had a particular affinity for Plato, St. Augustine, Pascal, and Kierkegaard, returning to them for inspiration throughout her life.

In addition to her many years at Hunter College, she taught at several other institutions, including the Catechetical Institute of St. Joseph's Seminary, Dunwoodie, New York; Franciscan University of Steubenville (where she served on the board of trustees for thirteen years); the Thomas More Institute in Rome; Ave Maria College in Michigan; and the Notre Dame Institute in Arlington, Virginia. She served on the board of Veil of Innocence and lent her support to innumerable Catholic apostolates and causes. Throughout her career she received numerous awards and three honorary degrees, including from Franciscan University. In 2013, she was invested Dame Grand Cross of the Equestrian Order of St. Gregory for her dedicated witness and leadership within the Catholic Church.

Lily became a household name through her early

association with Mother Angelica and EWTN. She made over eighty appearances on EWTN, including two series with Fr. Benedict Groeschel, C.F.R.: *Suffering and What to Do With It* and *Man and Woman: A Divine Invention*.

After Dietrich's death, she saw her primary mission to be the preservation of his legacy. In 2001, she published *The Soul of a Lion*, a biography based on Dietrich's memoirs. She also devoted two EWTN series to her husband's life: *A Knight for Truth* with Thomas Howard, and *He Dared Speak the Truth* with John Henry Crosby. In 2004, she joined John Henry Crosby and John F. Crosby to establish the Hildebrand Project as a vehicle for perpetuating her husband's legacy. She was particularly instrumental in inviting the support of Joseph Cardinal Ratzinger/Benedict XVI, which proved crucial for the Hildebrand Project. She worked closely with John Henry in the production of *My Battle Against Hitler*, featuring her husband's memoirs and anti-Nazi essays. She also worked closely with John Henry in writing her own *Memoirs of a Happy Failure*.

Lily is survived by her sister Marie Laure ("Flotte") Gillis (b. 1928) as well as thirteen nieces and nephews and their children. She is predeceased by her father Henri Jourdain (1892–1972) and mother Marthe (née van der Vorst) Jourdain (1899–1976), her brother Robert (1921–1961), and sisters Marie-Hélène ("Louloute") Peeters (1922–2018) and Christiane ("Titane") Jourdain (1935–2015).

ACKNOWLEDGEMENTS

Alice (Lily) von Hildebrand knew that friendship is a remnant of paradise, not just as a matter of philosophical insight, but from rich firsthand experience. She had a special talent for friendship and she possessed that deep interest in the other without which friendship cannot exist. Indeed, wherever she went, people soon felt able to pour out their hearts to Lily, who reciprocated with love, humor, and compassion. It would be impossible to thank here all of the people whom Lily would surely thank—they are too numerous for us to count!—but Lily encouraged us to say "Thank you" as much as we can, and so we shall try.

A number of individuals call for particular recognition. Alice Ann and Edward Grayson have for years championed the Hildebrand Project's efforts to promote Lily's work; they enabled the creation of alicevonhildebrand.org and their support is critical for the appearance of this volume. No one has supported the Hildebrand Project more significantly than Robert Luddy, who discovered Dietrich von Hildebrand by befriending Lily. The late Madeleine F. Stebbins was not just the incarnation of hospitality, but gave generously of her vast understanding that came from having been a student of Dietrich von Hildebrand and Lily's closest friend for nearly eighty years.

The appearance of this collection is a fruit of the Hildebrand Project in 2004, whose original and continuing financial supporters were among Lily's inner circle of friends, students, and admirers. In a special way we thank Edwin and Pat Bercier III, Stephen and Stephanie Block, Hedy K. Boelte, Anthony Brenninkmeyer, Evelyn Burg, Raymond Leo Cardinal Burke, Ellen A. Carney, Eva M. Cestari, Ronda Chervin, James V. Coffey, Sheila A. Conforti, Daniel and Teresa Cotter, Madeline L. Cottrell, Carol Cuddeback, Douglas and Leni Dewey, Michael and Suzanne Doherty, Doris E. Fader, Maria Fedoryka and Roy Schoeman, James & Helen Fitzgerald, Marylouise McGraw George, Dana Gioia, Rabbi Mark Gottlieb, Daniel and Rosalind Grimm, Karen Hanley, James A. Harold, Mary Healy, Fr. Brian W. Harrison, Julia Harrison, Nicholas and Jane Healy, Barbara B. Henkels, Roy and Elizabeth Heyne, Thomas Howard, Robert D. Hurt, Timothy and Nancy Joyce, Doug Keck, Betty Kelly, Robert Kreppel, Robert Levine, Marcel and Susan Lipkowitz, Paul and Dorothy Lochak, Patricia C. Lynch, Franco and Carolyn Madan, Donald W. Maliniak, Marie Marra, Valerie E. Mastronardi, Lee Matherne Jr., Kris and Buzz McLaughlin, Joseph Meaney and Marie Cabaud Meaney, Judy Mead, Eric Metaxas, Freda Bein Muldoon, Beatrice Murgio, Barbara P. Murphy, Fr. Gerald E. Murray, Grace Natoli, Tom and Mary Nightingale, Therese O'Brien, Andrew and Barbara Parrish, Jeffrey and Mary Petrino, Bartolomé Ribas Ozonas and

Elisabeth Wannieck, Kathleen C. Schmiedicke, Stephen D. Schwarz, Christina Shelton, Rev. Robert F. Slesinski, Robert and Joan Smith, Zeb and Christie Stearns, Timothy and Louise Stebbins, Jonathan and Julia Marie Teichert, Katie and Jules van Schaijik, Richard and Margaret Wall, Katherine Weir, Fritz and Theresia Wenisch, Mercedes Arzu Wilson, and Gregory C. Woodward.

The Hildebrand Project is immensely blessed to have a dedicated group of donors who have provided major support over the years, including Howard and Roberta Ahmanson, Scott and Martha Blandford, Donald and Michele D'Amour, Sean Fieler, Frank and Sally Hanna, Richard and Vera Hough, Thomas and Mara Lehrman, Thomas S. Murphy, Sr., James and Mary Perry, Duncan C. Sahner, Daniel and Annie Schreck, Stanley Stillman, John Studzinski CBE, and Scott and Lannette Turicchi.

Last but not least, we want to thank all of you who contributed to our Alice von Hildebrand Initiative, one of the fruits of which is this volume, and all of you who are sustaining benefactors. We warmly thank James Beauregard, Dana Marie Buchanan, Shannon Cagnina, Andrew D. Cannon, John F. Cannon, Daniel J. Cheely, Rafael Madan and Lilian Casas Foundation, Julia Calinescu, Allison Coates and Joshua Kneubuhl, Elaine C. Murphy, Susan F. Dane, Fr. Albert J. DeGiacomo, Norma Ehrenberg, Nicole C. Ehred, Ann English, Fr. Andrew Fryml, Fr. Donald Flumerfelt, John and Claire Foster, Fr. Adam Hertzfeld, Fr. David Hammond, Philip Harold, Michelle Hillaert, Shirley Haley, John Hanson, Linda M Holleran, Neal Howard, John Iverson, Timothy Jaeger, Patrick Jobst,

Shannon A. Joseph, Dolores S. Jarrell, John Kelly, Aloysius Ju Hyeok Kim, H. Kimberly Lukens, Christopher Lacaria, Ron Ledek, John J. Linn, Pamela Mardis, Marie E. Martin, Laura McCormick, Brent McAdam, Judy A. Miles, Gerard and Germana Mitchell, Brian and Juliane Mogck, Robert S. Mortenson Jr., Dennis B. Mulcare, Bill and Robin Mureiko, George Nolan, Kevin and Dawn O'Scannlain, Stephen and Jeanne Pavela, Claire Pinto, Jonna Rogers, Noah and Brittany Riner, William H. Rooney, Carl Rudorf, Fr. Zachary Swantek, Martha A. Sullivan, Raymond and Virginia St. Pierre, Kathleen C. Schmiedicke, Roy and Patricia Sheetz, Stan Sienkiewicz, Stephanie Stoeckl, Rose-Marie Fox-Shanahan, Ann Schmalstieg Barrett, Fr. Thomas W. Shaw Jr., Rosemary A. Tondra, Susan Treacy, Kathleen Tuthill, Larry A. Vaclavik, Tom Venzor, Paul White, Monica Zarandona.

Lily would want to thank each and every one of you personally, as she knew well that our work would not be possible without your generosity.

Made in the USA
Coppell, TX
07 November 2023

23921871R00105